I0800015

IMAGES
of America

PRICE

On the Cover: A freighter with a team of six horses prepares to leave Price with a loaded wagon train of goods. The full wagons are destined for Fort Duchesne and the Uintah-Ouray Ute Reservation, located northeast of Price. The freighter and his wagons would take the Nine Mile Canyon Road, a journey of five days in good weather, and return the same way with wagons loaded with Gilsonite. Freighters like this averaged 60¢ per 100 pounds of freight and only 50¢ per 100 pounds of Gilsonite. This photograph was taken around 1890. (Courtesy J. Frandsen Collection.)

IMAGES
of America

PRICE

SueAnn Martell, Darrin Teply, and
the Eastern Utah Tourism & History Association

ARCADIA
PUBLISHING

ISBN 978-1-4671-0506-4

Published by Arcadia Publishing
Charleston, South Carolina

Printed in the United States of America

Library of Congress Control Number: 2019957665

For all general information, please contact Arcadia Publishing:
Telephone 843-853-2070
Fax 843-853-0044
E-mail sales@arcadiapublishing.com
For customer service and orders:
Toll-Free 1-888-313-2665

Visit us on the Internet at www.arcadiapublishing.com

To those who fell along the way during the course of history. To those who made the history, not those that rewrite it. To those who preserve the history and keep it alive accurately.

CONTENTS

ACKNOWLEDGMENTS

A book project is not a one-man show. Many people over many years help in some small way to create a body of work. While far from comprehensive, we would like to thank several people for their help on this project.

Our hats are off and our hearts are full for the help that we have received over many years from Utah's foremost expert on Butch Cassidy and the Wild Bunch, the late Joel Frandsen. Prior to his death, Joel provided us with volumes of research, photographs, and personal recollections. It is our privilege to be able to share a fraction of that with you in this volume.

We would also like to thank Dr. Kenneth Carpenter, director of the Prehistoric Museum, Utah State University Eastern, for his gracious contribution of the photographs of the early museum.

Special thanks to Don Burge, Dr. Pam Miller, Dr. J. Eldon Dorman, and Dr. Susan Neel for always being the best teachers and friends and for being our personal cheerleaders.

A simple thank you is not enough for our support staff, Charlie, Lisa, Malea, Brianna, and Shelby Sweet; Zeph and BreAna Tucker; Beau Brinkerhoff; Chris Haycock; P.J. and Shawna Jensen; Matt and Georgina Nowak; Tiffani Baker; Dave Lowitz; Ernie and Nancy Bentley; Dan and Charlene Cummins; Danny and Doris Quinn; Todd Wilcox of My Side of the Universe Radio; and last but not least, the staff of JB's Restaurant. Be it physical labor, assistant tour guiding, or being a sounding board, you people keep us sane through our battles to keep history alive, interesting, and accurate.

We do not know where we would be without the loving support of our parents, George and Maurine Martell and Jim and Judith Teply, and our grandparents, James and Irene Greener, Jack and Phyllis Marchello, Walter and Catherine Martin, and Charlie and Myrtle Teply. Although they are gone, their support and encouragement continues.

We cannot thank our supporters enough! You have stuck with us through the bad times as well as the good times, and believe us, it has not gone unnoticed. From joining us on tours to taking the time to read our history to coming into our visitor center, you have all stepped up and made this worth it.

Finally, we would like to thank the first residents of Price—the ones who decided to stick it out and make Price a home. You, and your stories, will never be forgotten.

All photographs in the book are courtesy of the Eastern Utah Tourism & History Association Archival Collections unless otherwise noted.

INTRODUCTION

Located in east-central Utah, approximately 123 miles southeast of Salt Lake City, the Price River Valley of Carbon County is nestled between the Wasatch Plateau on the west and the Book Cliff Mountains to the north and east. With an average elevation of 6,000 feet above sea level, the Price River Valley enjoys a high desert climate with warm daytime temperatures and cold nighttime temperatures. It is a rough and unforgiving land, full of sagebrush and cactus, dry plateaus and mesas, and the riches of coal, natural gas, and oil underground.

Over 100 million years ago, dinosaurs called the area that would become Price home. They died and left their bones here in a treasure trove of prehistoric life. Eleven thousand years ago, during the Ice Age, mammoths and prehistoric hunters roamed the mountains. Shortly afterward, groups of Archaic people sought cave shelters and big game. It was the Fremont culture, living here 1,500 years ago, that left their mark as the first permanent settlers of the area. When they were gone, it was the Utes that called this area home. In the late 1870s, coal was discovered in the northern portion of Carbon County, and groups of settlers from neighboring Sanpete County ventured into the valley looking for grazing land.

The Price River Valley was one of the last places in Utah to be settled, and the Mormon pioneers who came to the banks of the Price River were skeptical that such a desolate land could be tamed. However, the potential for large fields of crops and the easy access to coal resources made up their minds for them, and they decided to stay. Once the railroad set their sights on Price, it became clear that it was a decision well made.

In the early 1880s, the Denver & Rio Grande Western Railroad began laying tracks for a railroad line to travel from Salt Lake City to Denver, Colorado. The plans took the railroad right through town, and seemingly overnight, Price became a railroad town. Encouraged by the work available, immigrants flocked to Price. Italians, Greeks, Slovenians, French, Chinese, Japanese, Irish, Mexicans, and dozens of other nationalities moved into Price and began to infuse their culture into that of the Utah desert.

Outlaws also joined the groups of people moving to Price. Butch Cassidy and Matt Warner, both Utah boys, used Price as a base for their operations. Warner liked the place so much that he put down roots, left the outlaw life (sort of), and became the law in town. In the late 1800s, Price was as rough-and-rowdy of an Old West town as one could find. Freighters and their empty wagons crowded the land near the railroad depot while they awaited the next load of freight to be moved to the Uintah Basin. Saloons and gambling halls were everywhere, and shootings were commonplace.

Though the time of the outlaw waned and the freighters were replaced by automobiles, the saloons, gambling halls, and houses of ill repute held on. These establishments provided much-needed revenue for Price, and these sporting houses and gentlemen's resort clubs were welcomed by the government of the town.

In 1911, under the direction of Mayor W.F. Olsen, Price was incorporated into a third-class city, and the town's dream of being known as "the Biggest Little City" was coming true. Restaurants, hotels, movie theaters, jewelry stores, furniture stores, dry goods, and mercantiles crowded together on Price's Main Street.

Mayor Olsen also sought to bring in revenue by welcoming tourism through the new concept of interstate highway travel. With automobiles becoming more available, paved highways were going to be the wave of the future. Price lobbied for the Lincoln Highway to pass through town, and it would have been successful, had Gov. William Spry not intervened and taken the road north. In time, the paved roads arrived, and so did the tourists, awed by the area's natural beauty.

While Price City flourished, there were times of trouble. Being surrounded by coal camps, Price was a center for both union and anti-union organizers. The United Mine Workers of America and the National Miners Union battled on the streets, and racial tensions soared. Italians and Greeks were just some of the groups targeted by hate. The Ku Klux Klan had a presence here. At the behest of law enforcement, martial law was declared many times, and National Guard troops were brought in to calm down the situation, many times too late. Fires, railroad accidents, mining disasters, and wars all took their toll on the town.

Always at the forefront of the early settler's minds was the need for a quality education system. While the first school in town was created by the initiative of Sally Ann Olsen, an official school board was soon established, and large, multi-grade schools were built. When the school board elected to build a countywide high school, it became a source of pride for not only Price, but also the surrounding mining camps. This Carbon High School took students from all nationalities and merged them together to create a dynamic, cultural mix that could only be found in a few other places.

The pinnacle of Price's effort to create quality education was in the mid-1930s, when it sought to create a college. Lobbying for a two-year junior college, the uphill battle with the state came to an end with the creation of Carbon College. The college merged the high school and the college to better prepare students to go on with their studies and earn advanced degrees. Today, Price is still a college town, with the college now under the guidance of Utah State University-Eastern. In addition to education, one of the themes that Price has always sought to develop was culture. Bands, both high school marching and orchestras as well as big band groups, made evenings in town a delight. The Silver Moon Dance Hall saw many parties, proms, and other festive occasions. The local movie theaters always showed the latest films from Hollywood as well as offered space for live performances and plays. Top actors and performers of the time came to Price to perform live.

In 1960, two men with a passion for the natural and historical beauty of the area dreamed into life what would become one of the best prehistoric museums in the nation. Don Burge and Dr. J. Eldon Dorman not only saw the potential of tourism dollars from such an attraction, but also desired to have a museum facility where people could learn about the past in a fun and entertaining way. Associated with the college, the museum opened in a tiny room and has since expanded to be a gem in the crown of Price.

From those humble beginnings with the first mud dugout on the banks of the Price River to a town that is the commercial center of Eastern Utah, Price has truly made a name for itself. Price, Utah, is diverse in a sea of common and rebellious in a field of conformity.

One

The Town that was God's Jumping-Off Point

By the early 1870s, the patch of desert that would be known as Price was inhabited by a rough and scattered collection of trappers, cattle rustlers, and explorers. The native Utes frequently traveled through the valley and used the area for hunting. In 1878, the first permanent settler finally called the Price River Valley home. Slowly, others arrived and set up their homesteads and farms. The Denver & Rio Grande Western Railroad laid down tracks through the Price River Valley beginning in 1879, and a full-fledged wood and desert rock town started to grow. A local census taken in 1882 showed that the population of the entire Price River Valley stood at just over 200 people.

Following the railroad as a tracklayer, Joseph Birch arrived in what would become Price and opened an eatery for the railroad construction workers. His young daughter, 19-year-old Isabella, was put to work cooking for the eatery. Isabella was quoted as saying, "This is God's jumping off place," as she attempted to gather a bucket of clean water from the Price River while she was repeatedly stabbed by the profusion of prickly pear cactus in the process, only to end up with a bucket of yellow mud for her trouble. Although disillusioned by the starkness of the valley, Isabella would go on to save the newly formed town of Price through her generosity.

Soon, Price was bustling with a busy railroad and a lucrative Gilsonite shipping center. Adding to the rich mixture were hotels, restaurants, saloons, and other businesses attracted by the proximity of the railroad. While the majority of the initial settlers were members of the Church of Jesus Christ of Latter-day Saints, the presence of the railroad infused the area with a wide variety of cultures, including Greek, Italian, French, and Chinese. These immigrants all flavored the area with their unique culture.

When Carbon County was carved out of the existing Emery County on March 8, 1894, Price was named as the county seat, and its position as the commercial center of Eastern Utah was set.

William Price II was a mercantile owner in the small town of Goshen, Utah. In exploring the area known as Spanish Fork Canyon in the early 1860s, Price came across a small river that he named the Price River. After naming the river, Price returned to Goshen, never to set foot in the valley or the town that would bear his name. Another legend claims the name comes from the railroad surveyor Thomas C. Price.

Yet another legend comes from the Denver & Rio Grande Western Railroad. When the railroad began laying track through the area, they dubbed the town Castle Valley Junction. The settlers in the area were known to raise the prices of goods when selling to the railroad. The railroad began calling the town "High Price," and the name was shortened to Price. This c. 1885 photograph shows the first of the permanent railroad depots built in Price.

While most travelers through the area of Price deemed the area as uninhabitable, pioneers from neighboring Sanpete County saw potential in the sagebrush-covered land. In the spring of 1878, pioneers Caleb Rhoades and Abraham Powell ventured into the Price River Valley on a trapping trip. They returned to their homes but vowed to settle the area permanently. One of the earliest cabins in Price is shown in this c. 1880 photograph.

Shown in the photograph are early Price settlers Caleb Baldwin Rhoades and his second wife, Sidsie Jensen Rhoades. One of the first settlers of Price, Caleb is also rumored to have discovered a rich gold mine in the Uintah Mountains of Utah, known as the Lost Rhoades Gold Mine. Caleb died on his ranch outside of Price on June 2, 1905, with the location of the gold mine a mystery. He is buried in the Price City Cemetery.

These first settlers to the Price River Valley were content to maintain an agricultural lifestyle, trying to get enough crops out of the harsh, high desert landscape with minimal water. Slowly, the focus on farming began to wane as the railroad brought more and more people to the valley and opened the way for a larger commercial center. This photograph shows an alfalfa field near Price around 1912.

This c. 1890 early view of Price shows the land office on the left and the 66 Saloon on the right, next to the Harmon Brothers Mercantile Company. The new location of the Price Co-Operative Mercantile is visible at center left in the photograph. A town landmark, Nickerson Hill is visible in the center of the photograph at the east end of Main Street.

In August 1883, the town of Price opened its first post office. Located on land owned by Fredrick A. Grames, the post office was housed in a rough, wooden shed along with Grames's general store. Grames was also made the first postmaster. Shortly after arriving in Price, Grames constructed a wooden bowery that he made available for anyone wanting to hold meetings or religious services.

As Price began to grow, one of the first areas of town to take shape was the commercial district. Located near the depot, early Main Street boasted several mercantiles. The Price Trading Company is shown here in 1890, shortly after its incorporation. The company officers were J.M. Whitmore, Alpha Ballinger, Charles Taylor, and Carlos Valentine. The Price Trading Company was built to provide competition to the Emery County Mercantile Company, also located near the depot.

Opened on March 30, 1887, the Emery County Mercantile Company was managed by future town president L.M. Olsen and provided both residents and visitors to Price with the best shopping experience. The Emery County Mercantile offered everything from farm implements to groceries and even oil paintings for a more beautiful home. This photograph was taken shortly after the store erected a new building in 1901.

After just a year and a half in its new store, the Emery County Mercantile was burned to the ground on September 20, 1903. The official cause of the fire was arson, and several broken windows and destroyed locked gates testified to an accelerant thrown into the building. Damage to the building was estimated at $50,000. No one was ever arrested for the crime, although all fingers pointed to a competing mercantile in the town. Mercantile president L.M. Olsen picked up stakes and moved to Ephraim, Utah, a year after the fire.

Fires plagued the newly growing town of Price. Not only was the town hit hard by the loss of the Emery County Mercantile, a fire on Main Street on October 21, 1911, destroyed several buildings. It seemed if one had a beef with a business owner, setting fire to his establishment was an adequate revenge. It also provided an opportunity for "business growth." The *Carbon County News* building was a total loss. In an unprecedented move, the competing *Eastern Utah Advocate* offered to produce and print the *Carbon County News* until the rival paper could get back on its feet.

As Price continued to grow, talk soon turned to creating a more comprehensive town. However, one man sought to undermine that plan. By using his homestead claim, Bishop George Frandsen formulated a plan to take over the land in the town and control it as a small Mormon agricultural community. In 1900, the town asked for help from an unlikely angel. This woman had not yet filed her claim, and if she could beat Frandsen to the land office in Salt Lake City, the town would be saved.

Isabella Birch Bryner was asked to use her claim. Arrangements were made for her to travel to Salt Lake City via a special "express" flat railroad car with a tent on it. Isabella filed her claim exactly 15 minutes before George Frandsen arrived. Isabella sold her claim to the town of Price for $2.50. She later claimed that she got a "really good corset" out of the deal. This photograph shows an artist's interpretation of the scene along with an inset of Isabella feeding her chickens.

Newspapers have always played an important part in Price's history. The first newspaper in Price was the *Eastern Utah Telegraph*, begun in 1891. It was purchased and renamed the *Eastern Utah Advocate* in 1895. By 1908, the *Carbon County News* arrived on the scene and merged with the *Eastern Utah Advocate* in 1915 to become the *News Advocate*. In 1915, the *Sun* began publishing until 1921 when it merged with the *News Advocate* and became the *Sun Advocate*. This c. 1915 photograph shows the *Advocate* building on Price's Main Street.

The newspapers of the early days of Price were extremely politically charged. The *Eastern Utah Advocate*, shown here around 1900, was one of the worst. Editor S.H. Brownlee terrorized not only the town's citizens, but also doomed his own paper from 1895 to 1897. Brownlee had been critical of numerous local officials and was removed as editor. In protest, Brownlee set the newspaper office on fire with minimal damage done and then later took over the newspaper office at gunpoint and spent hours destroying the equipment. This example shows that the quality of the *Advocate*'s newspaper and promotional photographs were not all that great either.

It was not uncommon to see small groups of the Ute tribe visiting and conducting business in Price. Price was the railroad connection to the Uintah Basin and supplied Fort Duchesne, located to the north of Price. Utes were forced onto the Uintah and Ouray Reservation near Fort Duchesne in the early 1880s, and numerous Utes made trips into Price for trade. The Ute visitors stayed in an area located south of the town of Price known as Indian Hills.

As the railroad presence increased and coal production in the nearby mountains picked up, immigrants flocked to Price. Most came looking for a better life than in their home countries of Italy, Greece, France, and Slovenia. Once they arrived, many found that mining was not to their liking, and they turned to more commercial pursuits. Located near the depot, the Pensione-Italiana, operated by Italian immigrant Joe Bonacci, offered homemade Italian meals and accommodations for travelers.

The Italian immigrants in Price worked hard to keep the culture that they brought with them. They also maintained their strong Catholic faith. The air in Price was thick with the delicious smells of Italian cooking from not only the many restaurants, but also from local kitchens. Here, an Italian immigrant family celebrates Christmas around 1910 the only way Italians can: with good food, homemade wine, and lots of family and friends.

The Greek immigrants also sought to keep their culture once they moved to Price. In this photograph, a Greek man poses in the traditional dress of a Greek soldier. In 1912, many Greeks residing in Price returned to their homeland to fight in the Balkan War. They returned with their weapons and used them to protect their fellow Greeks from harm in their new home.

Greek immigrants opened their own restaurants and their own controversial Greek coffeehouses in Price. The coffeehouses, like saloons, were places where Greek men could gather and enjoy drinks with their fellow countrymen. These coffeehouses were often targeted as illegal saloons, where drinking, smoking, and, potentially, labor talks were held. This c. 1910 photograph shows Greek men enjoying a day out.

As Price was first and foremost a railroad town, Chinese, Japanese, and Korean immigrants made the area their home as they sought work on the railroad. In the early 1900s, Price had two Japanese boardinghouses for Asian railroad workers, who maintained the tracks under the direction of an Irish foreman. These workers are using a handcar on the tracks near the Price depot.

Aside from the railroad, horses were the main mode of goods transportation in Price in the late 1800s and the early 1900s. Pioneer Livery & Feed Stables was one of several stables available in Price. Owner Elmore D. Shiner operated the stables until he took a job as a barn boss in charge of the horses and mules at the nearby Columbia coal mine.

Cowboy Jack Strange was a blacksmith in Price in the late 1890s. He soon took a job as a blacksmith with the US Calvary Buffalo Soldiers, operating out of nearby Fort Duchesne. Strange was known to ride along the Nine Mile Canyon Road between Price and Myton, Utah, assisting freighters and stagecoaches along the rough road. This commissioned photograph was taken by a Price photography studio in 1899 outside of town.

This c. 1919 photograph of west Main Street shows the thoroughly modern and up-to-date Savoy Hotel on the right. Because Price was the "Commercial Center of Eastern Utah" and "improved" roads were starting to connect the towns, people would stay at the fancy Savoy and shop the many car dealerships for their new vehicle. Visible in the next block is the Parker-Weeter Building (right) and the First National Bank (left), both of which are still standing today.

West Main Street in Price became the prosperity center of the town with the development of the north side of the street. Known as Banker's Row, the street boasted several banks, including the First National Bank of Price, the Carbon Emery Bank, and the Carbon County Bank, as well as other retail and entertainment establishments. The newly built Eko Theater is shown on the right in this 1912 photograph.

The first town hall in Price was a wooden affair built by the first town president, J.M. Whitmore, in 1893. Whitmore's successor, E.S. Horsley, commissioned this stone town hall during his term in 1895. The town hall included meeting facilities and places for plays and concerts as well as room for the newly established district court facilities.

The 1914–1915 Price officials posed for an official portrait in the Price Town Hall. Pictured are, from left to right, (first row) McClure Wilson, council; A.W. McKinnon, council; Carlos Gunderson, mayor; James F. Pace, council; E.S. Horsley, council; and J.W. Loofbourow, council; (second row) L.A. Lauber, recorder; Albert Pace, superintendent of water; Albert J. Grames, sexton; A.J. Lee, justice of the peace; Dr. F.F. Fisk, physician; F.E. Woods, attorney; D.J. Bryner, city marshal; J.H. Manson, electrician; and A.H. Hunten, city treasurer.

This 1916 photograph shows the governing council and mayor of Price City. From left to right are (first row) Albert Bryner, A.W. Horsley, A.Z. Marshall, and Margaret Horsley; (second row) A.D. Sutton, R.W. Crockett, Carlos Gunderson, Frank T. Bennett, Judge F.E. Woods, Robert McKune, and Carl R. Marcusen. This was also the World War I War Council for the Price area.

In 1902, Price held a celebration to honor the first pioneers that settled into the valley. The celebration was held at the Price Town Hall. One of the first settlers into the valley, Caleb Rhoades, is shown in this photograph at center right. Rhoades is holding the right corner of the banner that says, "Welcome to the Old Folks."

In 1894, the prominent citizens of Price wrote to Emery County requesting that Price be made into its own incorporated town. In the letter, they referenced a physical count of residents they completed in 1892. They boasted 308 people living in the town. A mere six years later, that number more than doubled to nearly 640 residents. A decade later, the US Census counted nearly 1,200 residents of the town. Price was on its way to becoming the economic center of Eastern Utah.

Two

The Town Built on Outlaw Gold

In the late 1800s and the early 1900s, the Price River Valley was very much the rowdy Old West. Outlaws used the town as a stopping point in their travels as well as the base of their operations throughout Eastern Utah. Bar fights, shootings in the streets, and robberies were common in the town. While some of them met their end in Price, for most of them, it was a safe haven. For the unfortunate outlaws that died in Price, they were all buried just outside of the gates of the cemetery in the town dump. This was an area reserved for the indigent, fallen women, and criminals. It was not until the mid-1970s during the expansion of the cemetery that their bodies were finally interred within the confines of sacred ground.

Butch Cassidy and his infamous Wild Bunch often traveled through town. While Cassidy never put down roots in Price, his best friend and mentor, Matt Warner, stayed. Warner not only moved to Price, he started a family and opened several businesses. He also became a lawman for the town and used much of his ill-gotten fortune to build up Price. In Warner's later years, he entertained several of his old outlaw friends at his home.

Warner was not the only outlaw to live in Price. His brother-in-law and fellow outlaw Tom McCarty was also a resident of Price. Lesser-known outlaw Joe Walker called Price home. Clarence L. "Gunplay" Maxwell, a "some-what member" of the Wild Bunch and longtime Price resident, was murdered on the street in Price by a hired assassin "employed" as a deputy sheriff. Mark P. Braffet, attorney for the Utah Fuel Company, was a businessman so hated among the residents of Price that he was nicknamed "King Braffet" and "the Carbon County Vampire."

With all of the businesses and properties built up by the stolen gold from the outlaws, Price was most certainly a town built with outlaw gold.

In the late 1800s and early 1900s, Price maintained the traditional "boom town" architecture with far more wooden storefronts than sturdy brick and rock structures. This photograph shows the south side of Main Street. The Price Drug Company anchored the left side of buildings while the 66 Saloon anchored the right side. The 66 Saloon was one of the wildest and deadliest bars in town, with numerous gunfights and stabbings taking place within its doors.

The north side of Main Street is shown here with the Price Co-Operative Mercantile on the right, the new Price Post Office next door, and at least two saloons occupying the rest of the block. A variety of townspeople came out for the c. 1900 photograph.

This photograph shows the extremely full Price–Vernal Stage departing from Price in 1900. Only a few of Eastern Utah's towns were connected by rail. The next best method of transportation was either one's own horse or an overloaded stagecoach. The Price–Vernal Stage ran through the remote Nine Mile Canyon, which was also through outlaw, Ute Indian, and buffalo soldier territory.

By 1913, the Main Street of Price was beginning to take on a more permanent look. The Price Co-Operative Mercantile was still there, as was the Price Post Office. The daily stage from Price to the Uintah Basin is shown here, arriving in town for a trip to Vernal and driven by a Mr. Watson. The stage line as well as the railroad offered many an outlaw the chance to travel freely between Price and other towns throughout Utah.

The local saloons offered drinking, gambling, and female companionship for both outlaws and lawmen. It was during these often heated games of chance that tempers flared, and guns were drawn. This c. 1890 photograph was taken in a saloon in Price. The staged photograph shows the act of cheating at cards and also how fast things can take a dramatic turn with a loaded pistol at the ready on the table.

In an effort to make people of the West feel safer from the threat of outlaws, railroad companies, banks, and detective agencies staged "robbery" and subsequently "capture" photographs. This photograph series was highly dramatized and often accompanied by the heroic lawmen swooping in and saving the day. This c. 1897 staged photograph was done by the Denver & Rio Grande Western Railroad. Notice how the train's fireman (far right) looks less than happy to be performing a "robbery."

Many members of Butch Cassidy's famous Wild Bunch passed through Price throughout their lifetimes. Butch Cassidy, seated right, found many friends in the Price River Valley who provided him and his men with fresh horses, a hot meal, and a safe place to stay. Taken in 1900 and known as "the Fort Worth Five," this photograph also shows, from left to right, Harry Longabaugh, William Carver, Ben Killpatrick, and Harvey Logan.

In one of the more daring crimes of the time, Butch Cassidy and his partner Elza Lay robbed the nearby Castle Gate mine payroll of nearly $8,000 in gold in April 1897. Cassidy and the Wild Bunch were never caught, and the gold was never recovered, but outlaw fever ran rampant throughout Eastern Utah. Some citizens and politicians alike were calling for the Wild Bunch to be captured at all costs. A $4,000 reward was placed on the head of Butch Cassidy, dead or alive. Elza, shown here in his younger days, had a reward of $3,000 on him. (Courtesy J. Frandsen Collection.)

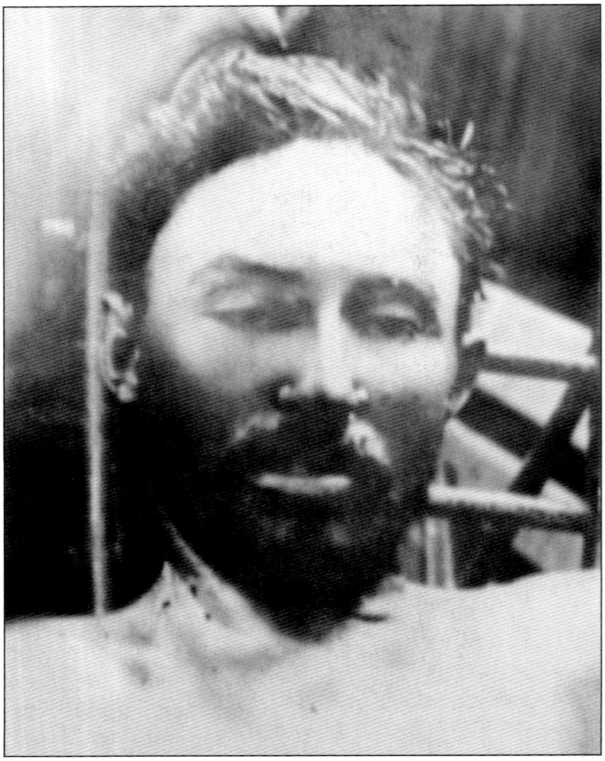

A causality of that outlaw fever was part-time member of the Wild Bunch Joe Walker. Walker played a small part in the success of the Castle Gate robbery by cutting the telegraph lines outside of Price. Walker was a relative of the Whitmores, a Utah cattle baron family, and repeatedly stole their cattle and horses as "payment" for a lost inheritance. This photograph shows Walker in death while on display at the Price depot in 1898. (Courtesy J. Frandsen Collection.)

Walker was rumored to be traveling with Butch Cassidy, and a posse of Price men was assembled a year later in May 1898. The posse was lured by the generous reward offered by the world-famous Pinkerton Detective Agency. Deep in the Book Cliff mountains, the 13-member posse came across Joe Walker, John Herring, and two other cowboys at their camp. This c. 1880 photograph shows Allan Pinkerton, seated at center of this promotional photograph.

Joe Walker and John Herring were murdered while asleep in their bedrolls. The posse tried to claim Herring was Cassidy in order to get the reward money of $4,000. The state was not fooled, and the bodies were exhumed several times over the next few weeks. Each posse member received $26.30 for their trouble. Walker and Herring's bodies became trapped in a "buried, and reburied, in Price" cycle that continues into the modern day. (Courtesy J. Frandsen Collection.)

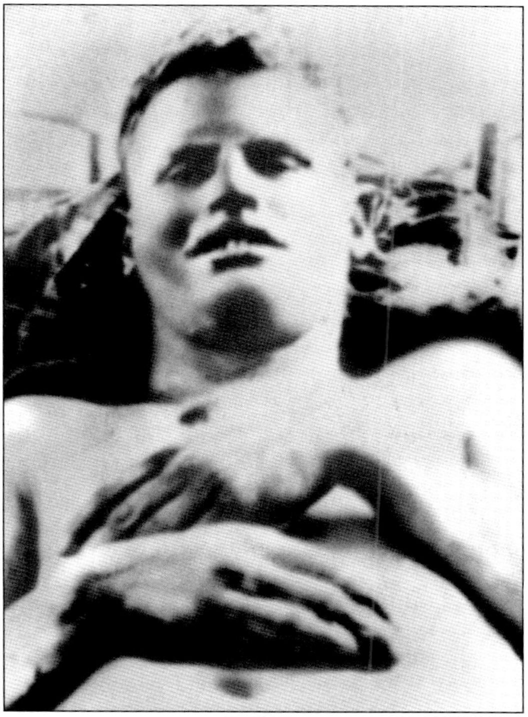

Carbon County sheriff Gustavus "Gus" Augustus Donant had the unfortunate luck to be the sheriff at the time that Butch Cassidy and Elza Lay robbed the nearby Pleasant Valley Coal Company. After repeatedly butting heads with the Carbon County commissioners and being denied reimbursement for using his own money in paying C.L. "Gunplay" Maxwell for his advance warning of the robbery, Donant was forced to resign under accusations by the Pleasant Valley Coal Company for dereliction of duties. (Courtesy J. Frandsen Collection.)

Emery County sheriff Azariah Tuttle Jr. had his own run-ins with the Wild Bunch as well as Carbon County sheriff Gus Donant. In late 1897, Sheriff Tuttle, being led by "Gunplay" Maxwell, cornered Joe Walker in a box canyon in the San Rafael Swell. Walker, aiming for Maxwell, shot Tuttle in the leg. Maxwell and the others in the party left Tuttle there and went to get help. Walker gave the badly injured Tuttle water before he escaped, leaving Tuttle to wait for rescue two days later.

Clarence L. Maxwell (right) found himself in Price in 1890. A geologist by trade, according to legend, Maxwell immediately ran afoul of the law, earning him the nickname "Gunplay." More of a swindler than an outright outlaw, Maxwell befriended powerful coal mine attorney Mark P. Braffet (left) and worked as Braffet's bodyguard. Maxwell still maintained ties to the Wild Bunch, all the while working a variety of lawman's jobs from mine guard to occasional deputy. (Courtesy J. Frandsen Collection.)

Carbon County sheriff deputy Edward Black Johnstone was still bitter after the Castle Gate payroll robbery. He saw Gunplay as nothing more than a member of the Butch Cassidy gang. Knowing he could not beat Maxwell in a fair gunfight, on August 23, 1909, Johnstone waited outside, shooting Maxwell twice in the back as he exited the 66 Saloon. Maxwell managed to turn around and get off one shot before Johnstone fired the fatal shot that murdered Gunplay in the street. This is Johnstone's "Hero" photograph, which ran in newspapers coast to coast. (Courtesy J. Frandsen Collection.)

Price mayor Rolla E. West remembered the shooting in his memoirs. West was a young man who built the coffin that held Gunplay. Maxwell's body was sent to Salt Lake City, where his second wife declined to take possession of it. Maxwell was "reclaimed" by Price, where he was buried in the city dump outside of the cemetery. In the early 1980s, his body was exhumed, and photographs were taken to prove it was indeed Maxwell. Certain members of the Carbon County elite have worked to destroy West's factual accounts and records of the events.

Born in the Utah town of Ephraim under the name of Willard Erastus Christianson, Matt Warner began his outlaw career rustling cattle. When he met Robert LeRoy Parker, another Utah boy, Warner and Butch Cassidy, as he had come to be known, became fast friends. Together, they robbed the Telluride Bank in Colorado. After Warner was caught in a plot to murder rival prospectors in Vernal, Utah, he served time in the Utah State Prison from 1896 to 1900. (Courtesy J. Frandsen Collection.)

While in prison, Matt Warner secured the services of attorney Mark P. Braffet. Warner told Braffet that once he was set free, he would like to set up a home in Price and become a law-abiding citizen. Speaking for Warner, Braffet relayed the message to Butch Cassidy, who was planning a jailbreak to get Warner free. This c. 1910 photograph shows Warner (standing right) and Braffet (seated right) in Price. (Courtesy J. Frandsen Collection.)

Matt Warner made good on his promise. With help from his brother-in-law Tom McCarty, pictured here, Warner built his first house in Price. He then ran for sheriff. The first time, he ran under his given name of Christianson and lost. The second time, he ran under his outlaw name of Warner and won by a landslide. (Courtesy J. Frandsen Collection.)

Mark P. Braffet was one of the most hated men in all of Eastern Utah. As attorney for the Utah Fuel Company, owners of the Winter Quarters, Castle Gate, and Sunnyside—Utah coal mines—Braffet was often accused of using his power to run roughshod over Price. He earned the unfortunate nickname of "King Braffet," and newspapers throughout the state saw him as a favorite target, especially the *News Advocate*.

Braffet and Warner teamed up to purchase land in Price and erected a large, two-story hotel, saloon, and restaurant next to the Price railroad depot. Called the Price Tavern, the building also housed a variety of businesses on its main floor and catered to business travelers on the railroad. After a series of personal tragedies and a brief bout of pneumonia, Braffet died at age 56 in his room at the Price Tavern on January 2, 1927.

Matt Warner built warehouses near the railroad depot. He owned and operated the Mint Saloon as well as the 66 Saloon and put money into his daughter and son-in-law's bar, John Causer's. Warner also had a bar that doubled as his courtroom in neighboring Carbonville when he was the justice of the peace there. This posed photograph shows Warner in his later years while he served as a lawman. (Courtesy J. Frandsen Collection.)

Matt Warner spent his life in Price doing what he always did. He ran cattle, operated businesses, and put a lot of money he could not account for into the town that he adopted. In his later years, Warner wrote a recollection serial for *Cosmopolitan* magazine detailing his time as a member of the Wild Bunch. It was made into a book in 1940. Matt died at his home on December 21, 1938. He is buried in Price. Sadly, much of the Warner history was taken from his daughter Joyce in her later years and never returned. Several local historians fought on Joyce Warner's behalf to get those materials back, as they were now being reclaimed and re-edited by other questionable dealings. (Courtesy J. Frandsen Collection.)

With the influx of outlaw gold into the building of Price, the town began to grow and live up to its self-given nickname, "the Biggest Little City." This photograph of Main Street shows many more stone buildings springing up throughout town, including the Wonder Store, a dry goods and notions store. This photograph was taken around 1900. (Courtesy J. Frandsen Collection.)

Though the age of the outlaw was coming to close by the mid-1900s, rough-and-tumble cowboys still roamed the streets of Price. Bryan Olsen, Ervin Fausett, and Butch Barlow pose for a c. 1912 photograph on the dirt streets of Price. The group is stopped in front of the land office on West Main Street.

While Price had a large number of banks in town and a large number of outlaws, the banks of Price were never a target for the outlaws of the area. Butch Cassidy and Matt Warner both taught the Wild Bunch that the local farmers, business owners, and residents were not to be harmed in their robberies. The local residents were seen as helpful to the outlaws and were rewarded for that help. This c. 1919 photograph shows a Main Street bustling with business and banks. By 1920, the days of masked outlaws robbing trains and banks and stealing cattle were over. Price was now a thoroughly modern city.

Three

THE TOWN SUSTAINED BY VICE

One would expect an early railroad town like Price to have its fair share of saloons, gambling halls, and brothels. One might not expect a progressive and modern town like Price in the mid-1900s to still have a large collection of vice. As Price grew, the money and taxes collected from these "illegal" industries were making a positive difference in the city's coffers.

In 1914, the Price City Police Department stationed police to stand in front of what the city termed "Gentlemen's Resort Clubs" and took down the names of all men entering and leaving the establishments. This practice continued until later that year when a court injunction demanded that the police stop the practice due to the harm caused to the businesses.

The first large-scale movement to clean up the vice problem was begun in 1932 when Rolla E. West, a former lawman, was elected as mayor of Price. West announced that he was assigning the police force to immediately clean out the brothels and gambling dens. In response, the city council overrode his action by slashing the chief of police's salary with the thinking that he could not do his job if he was not getting paid.

Then, in 1936, newly elected Price mayor J. Bracken Lee announced that instead of removing the vice from the town, he would embrace it. Lee saw the vice trade as a financial boon to the city and did everything in his power to keep it alive and well. Lee's controversial mayorship lasted 12 years, and although he made a great many enemies along the way, he went on to become governor of the State of Utah and then mayor of Salt Lake City.

A native of Price, J. Bracken Lee was elected as mayor of Price in 1935. Lee won the election by just two votes, and his claim to the office was challenged by incumbent B.W. Dalton. Lee assumed the mayor's chair at the first city council meeting of 1936 and was immediately threatened with arrest. It was not until the end of January 1936 that Lee was officially announced as the winner through a court decision.

In conservative Utah, Lee's view of vice was not popular. Lee passed measures that stated that drinking and prostitution were, in fact, legal within Price as long as the activities did not take place on the street. Within the numerous brothels throughout the business district of Price, working girls could "advertise" their presence as long as they were in second-floor windows. Gambling could take place in any business or residence as long as money was not exchanged. J. Bracken Lee's dry humor came through in this publicity photograph showing him learning how to "sweep things under the rug."

After 12 years as a popular mayor, Lee ran a successful campaign for governor of Utah. Opposition to Lee used his unique take on vice in his hometown to run a smear campaign against Lee. Under the direction of Lee's political rival, Gov. Herbert B. Maw, a pamphlet entitled "Morals and The Mayor" was distributed. In 1948, Lee defeated Maw and served two tumultuous terms as governor. This photograph shows J. Bracken Lee with his wife, Margaret Draper Lee, in front of the Utah governor's mansion.

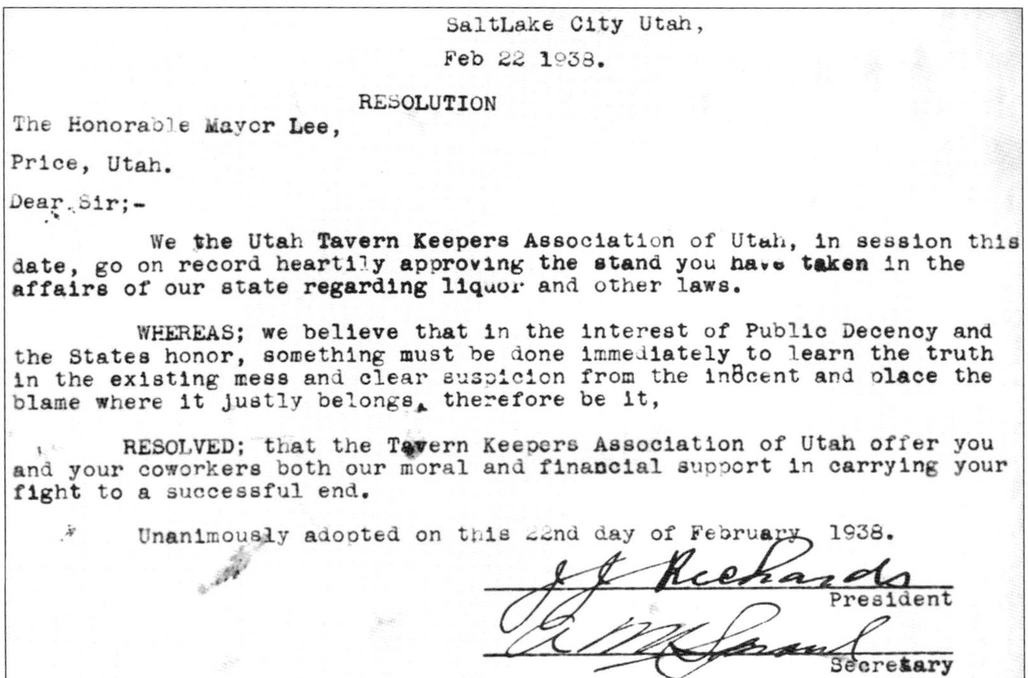

SaltLake City Utah,

Feb 22 1938.

RESOLUTION

The Honorable Mayor Lee,

Price, Utah.

Dear Sir;-

We the Utah Tavern Keepers Association of Utah, in session this date, go on record heartily approving the stand you have taken in the affairs of our state regarding liquor and other laws.

WHEREAS; we believe that in the interest of Public Decency and the States honor, something must be done immediately to learn the truth in the existing mess and clear suspicion from the inocent and place the blame where it justly belongs, therefore be it,

RESOLVED; that the Tavern Keepers Association of Utah offer you and your coworkers both our moral and financial support in carrying your fight to a successful end.

Unanimously adopted on this 22nd day of February 1938.

J. J. Richards
President

Secretary

While Lee was governor of Utah, he continued to provide "protection" of the vice trade in Price. He reportedly gave the saloon owners advance notice of raids that were planned on their locations from the Utah Department of Alcohol Beverage Control. These notices allowed the bar owners to hide their illegal liquor in plenty of time to avoid fines by the alcohol commission. This is a letter sent to Mayor J. Bracken Lee from the Utah Tavern Keepers Association in 1938.

After two successful terms as governor, J. Bracken Lee ran twice for US senator and lost both times. Then in 1960, Lee began two terms as mayor of Salt Lake City. Even though his political life moved away from Price, his loyalty to the people of Price never left him. This photograph from May 1955 shows Lee receiving the news that his battle with the Internal Revenue Service had taken a bad turn. One of Lee's most remembered quotes sums up his life, "Do it honestly, do it the best you know how, and let 'em holler."

In a bit of irony, J. Bracken Lee gifted beautifully carved crystal decanter sets to colleagues and friends after he had an unfortunate incident with liquor stored in an improperly cleaned wooden formaldehyde cask. This set was given to the authors' grandfather, James A. Greener. Lee and Greener were both members of the local Last Squad Club, a club for veterans of World War I. Lee and Greener were two of the final eight members of the club, with Lee ultimately being the final surviving member before dying on October 20, 1996.

Regardless of the city's stance on vice, the police department and the sheriff's office kept up their war on illegal bootlegging. In the 1920s, during the height of Prohibition, Carbon County sheriff Marion Bliss made it his personal mission to eradicate all bootlegging throughout the county. Bliss targeted immigrants trying to maintain their culture and was on record as being more than biased against other races and cultures. He always took promotional photographs of himself and his men with trophies of the raids. Notice that they are holding up a political cartoon.

Distilling operations took place all over the county. Sheriff Bliss located stills in basements and in the hillsides. One determined bootlegger, while being pursued by Bliss and his deputies, buried his automobile out in the desert and walked back into town. When the heat died down, he went back for the car and its load of illegal alcohol. Bliss was known to leave printed photographs of his other raids at known bootlegging locations as a calling card. This photograph shows, from left to right, Sheriff Bliss, Deputy Warren Peacock, and local physician Dr. J. Eldon Dorman.

At several times during Price's history, the town decided to go "dry," meaning that no alcohol could be sold within the city limits. In 1911, the first of the attempts at making Price a dry town took place. A statement by the *Eastern Utah Advocate* was, "If Price goes 'dry' in June, it will be dark by July." In an effort to keep that from happening, bootleggers stepped up and not only began making their own "moonshine," but with better transportation options, they could bring in alcohol from neighboring Colorado. This photograph shows some bootleggers performing repairs and sampling their products while using a dried stream bed as a roadway.

Bars and saloons were big business in Price. Some of the saloons included the 66, the Senate, the White House, and the Sideboard. French sheepman Pierre Jeanselme (center) was a business owner in Price catering to the French population of the town. A native of France, Jeanselme ran a successful business in town, the Farmer and Stockmen Store, as well as a bar. Future generations of the Jeanselmes ran a successful grocery store.

One of the authors' grandfathers, Italian immigrant John "Jack" Marchello, shown far right, made and sold his homemade wine to local saloons and bars. Marchello, a Northern Italian, utilized the tunnel systems in both Price and Helper until he refused to provide his "Dago Red" wine to a visiting Al Capone, a Southern Italian. Jack was turned out of the tunnels and charged with felony bootlegging by Sheriff Marion Bliss. Days before his public trial, charges were dropped when Prohibition was repealed, at which time Marchello had his own publicity photographs taken and sent them to Bliss.

The large population of immigrants within Price paid no attention to either national Prohibition laws or local law enforcement. Wine was a major part of their culture, and the making of homemade wine was an art form passed from generation to generation. Here, a group of Italian men shows off their homemade goods in this c. 1920 photograph.

Outlaw turned lawman Matt Warner owned his fair share of saloons in Price and the surrounding area, but he also had a financial stake in the bar known as John Causer's. Causer had married Hayda "Ada" Christianson, Warner's daughter from his first marriage to Rose Morgan. Causer not only owned the bar, but also dealt heavily in real estate in Price with the help and financial backing of Warner. This photograph shows a token that was used as money in Causer's bar.

Advertising was a huge part of early business, legal or otherwise, in Price. The Grill Cafe, located on West Main Street, used the ever popular matchbook to get its name out. While the 1920s-style art and the slogan "Where Particular People Dine" made the restaurant appealing, the real action in town was located in the basements of these establishments. Prohibition-era speakeasies were the underground spots for the best in drinking, gambling, and adult entertainment. However, the Grill Cafe did boast the "best beer in town."

Utah-brewed Fisher Beer had a wholesale distribution warehouse in Price operated by Clara Miller. The Price warehouse provided delivery of beer not only to places throughout Carbon County, but to neighboring Wasatch, Emery, Grand, and San Juan Counties as well, essentially all of southeastern Utah. This photograph was taken in 1935 and shows Miller's fleet of delivery trucks. The Kentucky Liquor House was another alcohol distributor in Price.

In true Old West style, one of the first buildings that visitors to the town saw was one of the numerous saloons. Most of the saloons, as well as the houses of ill repute, were located within a short walking distance of the Price railroad depot. This photograph shows a Denver & Rio Grande Western Railroad freight train pulling into Price, with an ever-present saloon in the background.

Between the years of 1912 and 1914, hotels were springing up all over Price. Two immigrant businessmen, Pietro Silvagni and Fred Paternoster, pictured, built two-story hotels on adjacent corners on today's Carbon Avenue. Silvagni and Paternoster both petitioned the city for a side entrance to their basements. After initially granting permission for the entrances, the city backpedaled and told the business owners that the entrances would not be allowed because they could lead to inappropriate activities in the basements. Both Silvagni and Paternoster ignored the city and built the entrances anyway. This photograph shows Paternoster in front of his business.

The first truly elaborate hotel, the Savoy, was built in Price in 1912. Built by Louis H. Lowenstein and partner Ben Stein, both Russian-Jewish immigrants to Price, the Savoy was touted as the second-finest hotel in the state. The Savoy was a three-story hotel with 51 rooms; 14 of those rooms had private baths with hot and cold running water. This photograph shows the hotel in the last stages of construction. The wagon was delivering furniture.

The Savoy was tastefully decorated with white ceilings and blue walls throughout the hotel. In the first few years after the hotel opened, the Carbon High School Orchestra performed on Friday and Saturday nights in the lobby. The hotel also had an on-premises barbershop, a bar, and a fully furnished pool hall in the basement. While the hotel maintained an air of elegance, gambling did take place. The Savoy burned down on January 18, 1965.

Located across the street from the rebuilt Price railroad depot and Mark Braffet's Tavern Hotel, the Carbon Hotel was a larger version of the Carbon Hotel and brothel located in neighboring Helper. The hotel offered its own bar as well as rooms for rent for the hour or the night.

Initially called the Eko Theater and built on Main Street in 1912, this c. 1940s photograph shows the Utah Theater. Renamed the Lyric Theater and then the Utah Theater, the Utah also showed x-rated movies after 11:00 p.m. This was a convenient location for these types of movies as there was brothel located right upstairs. Surprisingly, there was quite a bit of racy entertainment available for the big screen during the early days of film. Next door is the popular Silver Dollar Club, which tried to cultivate a female clientele.

Known previously as the Averill Hotel, the Ritz Hotel was the source of scandal in 1938 and 1939 when Utah liquor agents perjured themselves during a trial charging proprietor Sam Shortino of supplying them with liquor on the premises. During the trial, it was proven that Shortino had been in Salt Lake City at the time of the alleged crime. The liquor agents were sentenced to five years in prison, but their sentence was overturned by a Salt Lake City judge. The Ritz also had a two-lane bowling alley and small rooms in the basement that held only a drop-down bed, which blocked the door shut, keeping one in there with the working girl until your time was done.

While the lives of the working girls in Price were often difficult, Price City ordinance required the girls to be seen by a doctor once per week for a check-up. Their health—and subsequently, the health of their customers—was paramount in Price. These visits cost the owners of the so-called "Gentlemen's Resort Clubs" $25 per week. This shaky photograph shows several of these girls having a good time in front of the camera; it also proves that while male visitors were a dime a dozen, good photographers were harder to find.

Price Main Street, as well as other areas of town, are crisscrossed with the remains of its underground tunnels. These tunnels were used for a variety of reasons, but they mostly centered around Price's bootlegging, gambling, and prostitution industries. Some tunnels were large, brick affairs with light fixtures while others were no more than dirt walls and floors held back with lumber. This photograph shows a tunnel that ran underneath the Carbon County Courthouse on Main Street.

During the Cold War, this tunnel was converted to an improperly shielded fallout shelter and included sleeping areas and was well stocked with provisions, medicines, and legal books. It became the communications backbone for the building and had miles of wires running through it. The shelter could have held approximately 50 people uncomfortably. While the initial use of the tunnel is unknown, and it was not used during the Cold War, the sheriff's department often used the tunnel as a shooting range to pass the time between court cases.

Following Mayor J. Bracken Lee's directives about vice not being visible along the street, most businesses kept their gambling devices in basement saloons. In the 1940s, the Utah state attorney general and future governor of Utah, Calvin L. Rampton, led a raid on Price and confiscated over 150 slot machines and numerous roulette wheels. According to witnesses, the machines were lined up down Main Street "as far as the eye could see" before they were destroyed.

Four

The Town Expanded by Progress

By the turn of the 20th century, Price was growing by leaps and bounds. The initial dream of Price becoming another agricultural center in Utah was long gone as the Denver & Rio Grande Western Railroad began creating a commercial center. Wool from the Greek sheep farmers, dry goods, and supplies were moving to and from Price on a daily basis.

One of the largest cash producers was a waxy hydrocarbon from the nearby Uintah Basin. Known as Gilsonite for the original founder, Samuel H. Gilson, Gilsonite was used in everything from boot black to the classic Ford Model T black paint. With no railroads serving the Uintah Basin at that time, the closest rail hub was in Price. Teams of wagons made the arduous trip over the nearby Nine Mile Canyon road to take supplies to the basin and bring back loaded wagons of Gilsonite.

As transportation improved, so did Price. Regional commercial booster club and promoter Good Highway Boosterism fought for the transcontinental Lincoln Highway to pass through Price. The Lincoln Highway planned to link all of the Main Streets across America. Due to the State of Utah government backstabbing, the Lincoln Highway came through briefly and was classified as the 1913 Gravel Route. Price tried to adopt many other national highways in an effort to become more than a dirty speck on a desert map.

More businesses sprang up, providing a much wider variety of shopping opportunities and a wider sense of civilization than the previous selection of saloons, hotels, and restaurants. Price was beginning to take on a much more permanent appearance. It was certainly becoming clear that Price as the commercial center of Eastern Utah was here to stay.

In 1888, Samuel H. Gilson began the first large-scale commercial operation of Gilsonite mining in the nearby Uintah Basin. The company, through the Price Co-Operative Mercantile, employed dozens of men to haul freight and Gilsonite. While waiting for loads, the drovers, as they were called, stayed in an area near the Price depot. Known as "the Campground," locals and officials complained about the area, saying "the horses and mules are dirty, smelly and loud, and the drovers are worse."

The Greek sheepmen also took advantage of the services of the drovers and the railroad. They would come into town with wagonloads of wool to sell and trade. They would also have sheep drives in the spring and fall in order to buy and sell their sheep. This c. 1900 photograph shows a group of sheepmen bringing bags of wool into Price in front of the Price Co-Operative Mercantile.

As technology advanced and automobiles became more and more common, the freighters were replaced by auto lines. One of the biggest complaints from the freighters was the poor condition of the roads and the fact that in the best of conditions, it was a five-day trip from Price to the Uintah Basin. By 1908, auto lines were even providing taxi service to the outlying communities of both Carbon and neighboring Emery Counties. This photograph was taken around 1910 in front of the Anchor Auto Line on Main Street.

Even though arguably better than riding in a stagecoach or freight wagon, sometimes the trips in the auto lines were not the best. The roads were nothing more than horse trails with no accommodations for poor weather. This photograph shows the Berg Touring Car used by the Price Transportation Company in 1927. The company was owned and operated by B.F. McIntire and provided transportation to outlying coal camps around Price.

The worst of the driving was done during the winter, as illustrated in this photograph taken in 1927 on the road to the Consumers mining camp. Not only did the transportation companies offer public transport, but they also obtained the government contract to carry the mail to the coal camps. Driver Joe Prettyman had a busy day of digging in order to get back on the road.

With the increase in automobile traffic, both commercial and private, the poor condition of the roads and increased traffic laws came to the forefront. An editorial in the *News Advocate* lamented that drivers were speeding down Main Street "at over eight miles per hour and that thousands of school children were in danger from the automotive menace." It was not until 1922 that Main Street would be paved under the administration of Mayor W.W. Jones. This c. 1910 photograph taken on Main Street shows that a person was more likely to be swept away in a flood than killed by speeding autos.

When the Lincoln Highway Association came through Price and announced that the town would be a hub of the highway, Mayor W.F. Olsen stated that there would be a completed highway by the time the association did its inaugural publicity drive. No mechanized equipment was available, so all work was done by manpower and horsepower. On the day of the inaugural drive, the mayor declared a holiday and asked every able-bodied man to throw shovels full of gravel in front of the association caravan, thus giving it the name, the Lincoln Highway 1913 Gravel Route. This designation was quickly taken away by a backroom deal between Utah governor William Spry and Browning Firearms of Ogden, Utah.

As more and more people in Price could afford automobiles, the popularity of auto excursions grew. Here, a group of enthusiasts traveled from Price to Huntington around 1916. The road, although narrow, was in fairly good shape, at least in this section. These early types of excursions were not all that different from modern off-road ATV and UTV rides with about the same amount of power coming from their machines.

In 1912, the Good Highways Movement was conceived. The goal was to unite all of the Main Streets in a continuous highway, linking all of the states from the East Coast to the West Coast, much like the transcontinental railroad connected towns across the country. Local chambers of commerce and business clubs jumped on board the movement and began a large-scale campaign of "boosterism." This c. 1940 photograph shows the members of the Carbon County Chamber of Commerce announcing their support for the new highway designations US Highway 6 and 50.

Much publicity surrounded the plans for the Lincoln Highway. Photographers flocked to the adventurous groups who traveled from state to state via auto and used their photographs to sway the decisions of the politicians who wanted the prestigious highway system to go through their own towns. After the gravel route designation was relocated by Governor Spry, Price fought to become a part of any highway system. The main problem was the primitive state of the desert roads. Some biased politicians even denied Price state improvement funds, claiming that they only wanted the paved highways so that alcohol could be smuggled easier.

The early auto road just outside of the famous landmark of Castle Gate, Utah, nine miles northwest of Price, is pictured on a cold and dreary day around 1912. The road was an important connection between Price and Salt Lake City. This single-track, rutted road was later improved by outlaw-turned-lawman Matt Warner in an effort to make "alcohol commerce" easier. It became an example of "if the state won't give you your share of the money, you turn to those who will benefit from it to improve it," and Warner was already sinking his money into Price. This road has been further improved and is still in use today as the main road into Carbon County.

One of the main requirements of the new highway system was the road's proximity to existing railroad lines. If the cross-country motorist broke down or needed assistance in other ways, they could look to the railroad for help or alternative transportation. Many motorists were known to put their cars onto passing trains when the going got rough. This photograph shows a motorist seeking help on the road outside of Green River, Utah, on her way from Price.

One of the major sticking points with assigning the official Lincoln Highway designation to Price was the type of paving that was eventually done to the roads. Price fought for the now familiar asphalt treated roads instead of the 10-inch thick white cement roadway required by the Lincoln Highway Association (LHA). Price ran a nationwide media campaign complete with striking photographs of roads paved with Carbon County rock asphalt. The major complaint about the asphalt roads was that they could get one's car and shoes dirty.

All of these new cars moving in and out of the Price area meant big business for the men of Price. Several car dealerships and auto parts stores opened along Main Street. This c. 1918 photograph shows the interior of the Redd Auto Supplies Store on West Main Street. The store carried all of the supplies needed for any cross-country trip.

Not only could one buy auto supplies, the Redd-Culp Motor Company next door sold the latest in automobiles. A Ford Model T Touring Car could be purchased in 1918 for around $360; however, the average household income was just over $1,500 per year. It was a pricey investment.

Along with auto suppliers and dealerships, gas stations began sprouting up all over Price. Here, the Utah Oil Refining Company, located next door to the Redd-Culp Motor Company, opened a service station specializing in locally sourced crude oil. The crude came from a well called "the Success" and was located east of Price in a geologic area known as Farnham Dome.

On the eastern end of Main Street, Fred's Service offered gas, auto supplies, and clean restrooms. Originally located on West Main Street, Fred's Service opened in 1936 and was owned and operated by Fred Bonomo and Verdell Pace. In 1945, Bonomo relocated Fred's Service to a new building across from the Price City Hall. This photograph was taken just after the station opened in its new location.

Johnson Service opened in the mid-1930s and offered a one-stop service for all automobile needs. Located on the corner of 100 West and Main Streets, Johnson Service was owned and operated by A.E. Johnson. This photograph shows the station in the 1940s with the Utah Oil Refining Company station just visible at left.

While automobiles were becoming all the rage in transportation, the railroad was also booming. However, on the night of June 22, 1910, the depot built in the 1880s caught fire from sparks thrown from an idling train and was a total loss. Looking to increase the size of the depot, the railroad made the decision to move it east. Price officials balked at the idea saying the depot was the center of town and could not be moved. This photograph shows the new Price depot shortly after completion in 1911.

While the Denver & Rio Grande Western Railroad was looking for a place to build its new depot, attorney and businessman Mark P. Braffet offered to let the railroad use space in his soon to be completed Price Tavern—for a fee, of course. The railroad refused and instead built its new depot next door to Braffet's establishment. This c. 1915 photograph shows how popular the train was as a mode of transportation in Price.

With the new depot moving eastward by two blocks, the center of town moved with it. In fact, the whole town underwent a radical renaming of the streets in 1926. During the administration of Mayor C.H. Madsen, streets that had been named with letters of the alphabet on the west to east streets and numbers on south to north streets were renamed with a more coordinate-based system. Carbon Avenue and Main Street became the center of town. Prior to 1926, Carbon Avenue was called Eighth Street, and Main Street was known as I Street. This c. 1926 photograph shows the new Price Depot at right.

The Denver & Rio Grande Western Railroad was not the only railroad in town to operate a depot. In 1908 and 1909, respectively, the Southern Utah Railroad and the Castle Valley Railroad sought to run railroad lines from Price to the coal camps of Hiawatha and Mohrland, south of Price. Because of the close proximity of the two camps, the railroads came to a deal where they would share trackage rights and a depot. Their depot was located just east of the Denver & Rio Grande Western's depot. This c. 1911 photograph shows the depot.

While the main purpose of the combined Southern Utah and Castle Valley Railroads was to move vast quantities of coal from the mining areas south of Price, they also dealt in passenger traffic. People could purchase a passenger ticket and travel back and forth from Hiawatha or Mohrland on an every other day schedule. The passenger coach for the railroad was a used car from the Bamberger Electric Railroad. This c. 1920s photograph shows the combined depot behind tracks of loaded coal cars.

Train travel and travel by car were not the only forms of transportation available in the growing town of Price. In 1933, Price opened a regional airport with service to Salt Lake City and Grand Junction, Colorado. The airport was backed by the Carbon County Chamber of Commerce, with coal mining magnate George Schultz as a major supporter. The airport was managed by James A. Lund and offered passenger flights and student instruction.

In 1910, Price contracted with a private company to provide electricity and lights to Price. Former Price treasurer Alpha Ballinger was awarded the contract to build a power station and supply all poles and wires necessary for the production of electricity. Ballinger then agreed to supply Price with 10 modern arch lights for Main Street. Although the contract was signed for 50 years, Price City took over the operation of the power plant in 1918. This c. 1911 photograph shows the interior of Ballinger's power plant.

By 1922, Price had installed its first "white way" along Main Street. The illumination of city streets was a novel concept and one that was heavily promoted. Mayor W.W. Jones not only saw the project to completion, but also paved Main Street for the first time during his one-year administration. This linen postcard shows Price City's electric Main Street in the late 1930s.

While the telephone had been in use in Price since 1891, the explosion of telephones in people's homes and businesses did not fully come around until the early 1900s. Price had its own telephone office where operators connected the calls and took messages for phone customers. This photograph shows the telephone office in Price in the early 1920s.

In 1926, Price City appointed a Price City Hospital Board to construct and oversee a city hospital. It was the first hospital in the city. Health care had been previously provided by doctors in the patients' own homes or their modest offices. This photograph shows a band concert organized by the nurses at the hospital in 1926. The nurses closed the porch with muslin curtains and made cakes for the children in the hospital to eat while they enjoyed the concert. There were seven children at the hospital at the time.

This photograph shows the nurses of the Price City Hospital, two of their patients, and the patients' mothers. The boy on crutches was named Tony and had a broken femur. The boy in the wheelchair spent a year at the hospital recovering from a ruptured appendix. His mother, standing behind him, decorated the entire hospital for Christmas so he and the other patients would have a good holiday. The photograph was taken in 1927.

In 1933, plans were under way for a larger, more advanced hospital in Price. Money was tight, and it was not until 1934 when one of the most prominent doctors in Price passed away that a new hospital began. Dr. F.F. Fisk bequeathed a total of $356,000 in cash and property toward the construction of a new hospital. The hospital was built by the Works Progress Administration (WPA) and was constructed in the shape of a capital *H*. The building was constructed north of the city park.

During the Great Depression, the US government established the Civilian Conservation Corps (CCC). The CCC was a voluntary work group for single, unemployed men ages 17 to 28. The CCC established a camp in Price as well as one in nearby Ferron. The Price camp was classified as SCS-3 and responsible for soil conservation activities. This c. 1936 photograph shows an overview of the camp, which was located near the cemetery.

The men at Price camp pose for a photograph in October 1936. The photograph includes the cooks as well as the commanders of the camp. The CCC provided these men with lodging, food, and clothing and paid them $30 per month in wages. Of that $30, a total of $25 had to be sent home to the men's families. The CCC was in operation from 1933 until World War II required the closing of the project.

At the end of World War II, the United States was facing a severe housing shortage. To remedy that problem, Pres. Harry S. Truman implemented the Reconversion Housing Project in 1946. Under the project, houses would be built, and the first choice of those homes would be given to returning veterans of World War II. The project was undertaken in Price in the area near the cemetery and the new college.

The housing project built homes for veterans that they could purchase for a maximum of $10,000 or rent for an average of $80 per month. This photograph shows the homes under construction near the cemetery, approximately one mile northeast of Main Street, in 1947. The Reconversion Housing Project ended on December 31, 1947.

In an effort to bring more people into Price, the Park Dale Townsite Company, owned by Emmett K. Olsen, mass printed tabloid-sized advertising sheets featuring giant photographs on glossy clay-baked newspaper and sent them throughout the region. These photographs showed all aspects of life in Price and its surrounding area. With its office located in the Eko Theater building on Main Street, Olsen also had the perfect opportunity to promote his own apartment building known as Olsen Flats.

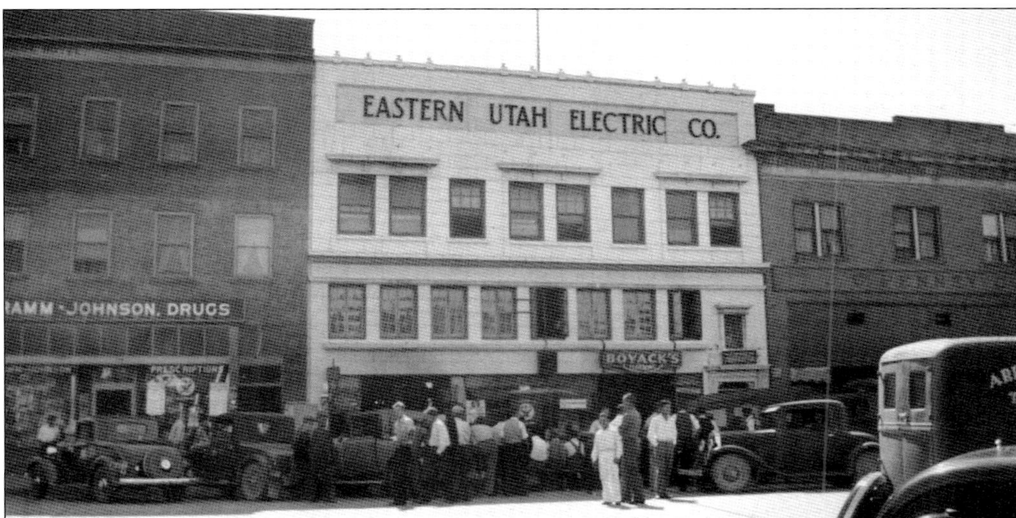

Despite the name, the Eastern Utah Electric Company was much more than just light fixtures. It sold tires; automobile repair tools; fishing, camping, and hunting supplies; and the latest in radio and later television sets. This c. 1936 photograph shows a group of men assembled at the store for a radio broadcast that was played on the sidewalk for anyone who wanted to listen. The company also provided radio sets to Carbon High School for important events like election results. The store shared space with Boyack's Men Clothing and was located next to Schramm-Johnson Drug Store and the J.C. Penney Company.

One of the oldest, continuously operated businesses in Price, Oliveto's Store was opened on October 12, 1935, by Italian immigrants Louis and Elena Oliveto. The Olivetos offered a wide variety of home furnishings and appliances. They also offered home delivery. This photograph shows Louis Oliveto posing by his delivery truck after the store's 1935 grand opening.

Prior to opening a store in Price, Louis Oliveto owned and operated a general merchandise store in nearby Sunnyside, Utah. Louis and Elena Oliveto had a little bit of everything in their store. This photograph, taken on its grand opening in 1935, shows a large selection of dishes, cookware, toys, cleaning supplies, and other household necessities. The store is still in operation by the Oliveto family in the same location as it was in 1935.

Located on the east end of Main Street, the Towne Cafe and Bakery was owned and operated by John Spatafore and his family. When the restaurant opened in 1950, the first advertisement included this verse: "There was a city named Price, Which as a town was exceptionally nice, But there was one thing it was needin', A good place to eat in, And we sure put this problem on ice!" The restaurant was open 24 hours a day and could seat 200 in the dining room. It catered to clubs and organizations. The restaurant burned down in the mid-1980s.

As Price grew, the town became more and more like the city's dream of becoming the largest commercial center between Denver and Salt Lake City. In 1920, the population of Price stood at just less than 3,000 residents. In 1930, it had grown to 5,200, and by 1940, the population of Price was at 6,500. This c. 1930 photograph shows West Main Street with its large selection of automobile dealerships and service garages.

In 1943, Price purchased a new fire truck for $5,000. This truck was state of the art in every way and provided better fire suppression for the growing town. This photograph shows members of the Price City Fire Department and their wives taking the new truck for a joyride down West Main Street. Across the street is the Price Hotel, the Carbon-Emery Market, the Stockman's Club, the Tip Top Bar, and the Grill Cafe.

In 1912, Mayor W.F. Olsen secured a grant for the construction of a Carnegie Library in Price. Philanthropist Andrew Carnegie gifted money for libraries to be built in towns all over the world. The library was constructed, and a library board appointed. Ivy Lowery was the first librarian. Lowery received a salary of $25 per month, and the library was open from 3:00 p.m. to 9:00 p.m. six days a week. This c. 1930 photograph shows the Carnegie Library next to the Price City Hall.

While J. Bracken Lee's 12 years as mayor of Price was filled with criticism, he also accomplished much in the way of improvements to the town. In 1937, Lee demolished the Price City Hall, built in 1895 and remodeled in 1921, to make way for a new $4 million city hall and auditorium. This photograph shows, from left to right, George Collingham, William Grogan, Albert J. Grames, Councilmen Sheldon L. Anderson, John W. Holden, E.N. Chidester, W.E. McIntire, Mayor J. Bracken Lee, Carlyle Pace, Arthur W. Horsely, Arthur N. Smith, and Ralph P. Anderson.

In February 1938, Price's new state-of-the-art city hall was opened. The building included a gymnasium, the fire station, and a civic auditorium, its crowning glory. The auditorium was designed and decorated in an Art Deco style, complete with theatrical gargoyles above the stage. The auditorium initially accommodated 300 people on the main floor and an additional 200 in the balcony. City leaders were pleased with the auditorium, claiming that the facility would be the "best in the Intermountain West."

Once completed, the new Price City Hall, Auditorium, and Municipal Building added a nice, modern touch to the block. This aerial photograph, taken shortly after the building was finished, shows the city hall on the right, the Carnegie Library next to it on the left, and the Price Latter-day Saints Tabernacle and Tithing House on the far left. At the rear left of the photograph is the Price Central School, and at rear right is the Harding School.

With the completion of the Price Airport and the popularity of privately owned aircraft, aerial photographs of the city became common. This c. 1937 photograph shows Carbon High School, the junior high school, and outlying buildings at the top of Carbon Avenue. It also shows the city park, the newly completed *H*-shaped hospital, the irrigation canal in front of the high school, the cemetery, and the CCC camp at the top of the photograph.

This view is looking south from Carbon High School toward Main Street and the railroad lines. At the center left of the photograph is the Carnegie Library, the Church of Jesus Christ of Latter-day Saints (LDS) Tabernacle, and Central and Harding Schools. On the right is Carbon Avenue leading out of Price south toward neighboring Emery County. Mark P. Braffet's Price Tavern is visible next to the railroad crossing at Carbon Avenue, and the Price Depot is located to the left of the tavern. Main Street is one block north of the railroad crossing.

At the left center of the photograph is the Price City Municipal Complex. The Price City Hall has been demolished to prepare for the construction of J. Bracken Lee's new city hall. A footpath is visible between the Harding School and the Central School in the same block. The Price River is seen in the upper right of the photograph.

This view is looking toward the north. Price City Park is shown at left center, and the *H*-shaped hospital is just to the north of the park. The track for the high school is shown at right center. The housing development north of the hospital is the Park Dale Townsite, planned and developed by Emmett K. Olsen and the Park Dale Reservoir; it is shown in the upper left of the photograph.

While Carbon High School had its own indoor swimming pool, a public swimming pool had been on the wish list of Price for some time. In 1921, the local Boy Scouts approached the city about turning an abandoned reservoir into a pool with bathing houses. While primitive in nature, the pool was a huge success. In 1925, the Price Rotary Club announced that it was going to build a concrete, outdoor swimming pool in a portion of the city park. This photograph shows an updated version of the swimming pool in 1950.

Completed in February 1931, the new Price Post Office was a project of the Works Progress Administration (WPA). The cornerstone for the building was laid in 1930. The building cost nearly $105,000 and took only six months to construct, but the process of acquiring a new post office had taken nearly nine years. The project was spearheaded by Utah congressman Don B. Colton, the town of Price, and the chamber of commerce. This photograph was taken around 1931. This post office is still in use.

Decked out in all of the town's patriotic finery, Price's Main Street was a hive of activity in this photograph taken around 1940. The photograph shows the Liberty Hotel, located on the corner of Main Street and Carbon Avenue; the Silvagni Building, located on the opposite corner (at left in the photograph); and the sign atop the Savoy Hotel, located on the left in the next block. Price had certainly achieved its goal as the commercial center of Eastern Utah.

When the Price railroad depot moved to Carbon Avenue, the center of town moved to the corner of Carbon Avenue and Main Street, shown here in 1961. Close proximity to the depot was key for any business in downtown. The businesses pictured are, from right to left, Quality Cleaners; the former Eko Theater, now for sale and called the Crown; the Silver Dollar Club; Elite Jewelry; and the clothing and housewares division of the Price Trading Company.

Taken around 1961, this view of Price's Main Street is looking southwest from the top of Nickerson Hill. Price had expanded well east of the main center of town. The mountains of the Wasatch Plateau as well as the high desert mesas and pinnacles that surround the town are visible in the background. Unlike most Old West boom towns, plucky little Price had held on and carved a city out of a little spot of dirt in the desert.

Five

The Town Rocked by Strife

All towns have their fair share of events that can rock the town to its core. These trying times can either sever a town to pieces or pull it tightly together. With Price being the largest town in eastern Utah and with a large and diverse population, turbulent times were inevitable.

Coal mining and railroad strikes fueled by corporate greed and racial tensions were commonplace. Many times these strikes became bloody, and as things were already tense, these events spilled over to the boiling point. One of these events resulted in the last official hanging of an African American in the state of Utah. The lynching drew over 500 men, women, and children to the scene, many of whom brought blankets and picnic lunches and made a day of it. High-profile court cases were heard here, and people were polarized with the biased outcomes. Martial law was declared more than once to try to control the population and keep the peace.

Accidents along the railroad killed dozens of people over the years; some were beloved citizens of the town. Former town president James M. Whitmore was run over by a passenger train near his home at the age of 65. The entire town shut down for the funeral, and former Utah state governor William Spry attended the service.

Through all of the turmoil, Price always managed to rebound, and overall, the good times truly outnumbered all the bad. A melting pot of cultures, Price lived through its growing pains and eventually became one of the most culturally complete cities in Utah.

One of the most dastardly characters in Price history was J.W. Warf. Claiming that he had a college degree in both geology and law before he was 18 years old, Warf was appointed as county attorney for Carbon County. Warf was a part of the posse that killed Joe Walker and John Herring. On July 23, 1898, Warf killed fellow posse member Jack Watson by firing his revolver up Watson's backside while they were in the Senate Saloon on Main Street. Warf was let go on a plea of self-defense.

Part-time Texas Ranger and part-time drunk gambler, Jack Watson was sent to Price by the infamous lawman Doc Shores to clean up the outlaws that were stealing from Utah cattle baron Preston Nutter. After the successful posse run to kill members of the Wild Bunch, Watson wanted his reward money. J.W. Warf and city treasuer Alpha Ballinger beat Watson nearly to death in order to get Watson's portion of the reward. Seeking revenge in a bottle, Watson was drinking in the Senate Saloon when he was shot and murdered by Warf. Watson's share of the reward was claimed but not by Watson or his family—both shares were claimed by Warf.

Arguably one of the most powerful groups in Carbon County, the Utah Fuel Company, a subsidiary of the Pleasant Valley Coal Company, owned by the Denver & Rio Grande Western Railroad, was unilaterally hated throughout the area. This photograph from 1890 shows attorney Mark P. Braffet (front row with his eyes closed), Braffet's bodyguard, C.L. "Gunplay" Maxwell (seated second to the left from Braffet, with his hands crossed) and Maxwell's future killer, Deputy Edward Black Johnstone (standing directly behind Braffet, glaring at Maxwell). The dog's job at the meeting is not clear.

In a political cartoon published in a statewide newspaper, the Utah Fuel Company is portrayed as controlling the Carbon County court system with a heavy-handed, six-shooter approach. While the mining company operated coal mines throughout the county and in Colorado, it was accused of defrauding widows, squashing private businesses within the towns, running roughshod over the residents, and arresting striking miners without cause. Company attorney Mark P. Braffet is portrayed in the front of the cartoon.

A Long Range View of a Carbon County Courtroom.

One of the most iconic, and misidentified, photographs to come out of Price and Utah's history, this image captured Italian coal miners where they were imprisoned in Price. In the spring of 1904, the Utah Fuel Company used armed guards to round up striking miners in the middle of the night. The miners were then taken by train to Price, where they were placed inside one of the remaining outdoor sheds of the burned ruins of the Emery County Mercantile. The miners were allowed water from the river, and food was provided for them once per day by their own

families. The photograph shows C.L. "Gunplay" Maxwell (far left on a rock pile, holding a long gun), Mark P. Braffet (next to Maxwell in the long overcoat), and Deputy Edward Black Johnstone (second from right). The photograph has been repeatedly misidentified as the aftermath of the Wild Bunch robbery of the Castle Gate payroll. While some of the people in the photograph were undoubtedly present during the robbery, it took place a full six years before this coal mine strike, and the photograph was taken in Price.

During times of strikes and when word was floating around of a repeat of the payroll robbery, posses, lawmen, and hired thugs descended upon the area to try and keep the peace. Most of the time, the armed presence just caused further conflict. This was especially true when specific immigrant groups were targeted as union agitators. This c. 1897 photograph was taken in Castle Gate and shows an armed posse unloading from a Denver & Rio Grande Western Railroad train.

During the 1903–1904 coal mine strike, Price was visited by a woman known throughout the United States for helping striking miners and their families. Mary Harris Jones was given the name "Mother" as a title of respect from some of the thousands of miners she helped. Mother Jones addressed the citizens of Price and said she was there "to agitate, educate and aggravate." Mother Jones watched with horror as Italian miners were rounded up at gunpoint and brought to Price. She said, "Their crime was that they had struck against the power of gold."

Unions and worker's rights were always hot buttons of contention, and this was even more so in Price, which was not controlled by any mining company. Union organizers could freely gather in Price, as it was seen as neutral territory. This photograph shows a pro-Union march on Price's Main Street, led by the Carbon High School marching band. Some parents were so outraged that their children were used in such propaganda that they refused to let them march in any more parades in Price. This photograph was taken around 1933.

This is a dramatic still image from an early hand-cranked home movie camera. It was filmed from the second floor of a Main Street business and shows members of the allegedly communist-funded National Miners Union (NMU) marching into Price in an effort to secure the release of several of their members incarcerated in the Price jail at the courthouse. The furniture store, whose sign is just visible at left, suffered damage when the windows were hit and broken by a gas bomb and tear gas canisters launched by law enforcement just after this photograph was taken. This grainy footage was filmed on September 11, 1933. The actual events and the footage have been long denied by the State of Utah.

This is another frame from the same surviving camera footage. This scene shows the angry NMU members standing off with not only law officials and plain-clothed national guardsmen, but also hastily deputized adults and 15-year-old children, who were also given long guns. Other frames show tear gas canisters and gas bombs that were used to try and disperse the crowd while fire department water hoses were sprayed on the unarmed protesters, as the county had already been declared as belonging to the United Mine Workers Union (UMWA). Upon being assaulted, the peaceful march immediately turned violent, with women in the protest as well as the crowd slapping armed officers. Over the past 15 years, this footage has been censored, and the authors have some of the last surviving frames of the events. Few have seen all of the footage.

The NMU protesters were pushed back down Price's Main Street from the courthouse and led at gun point down the tracks back toward Helper by law enforcement and deputies. In preparation for another violent riot at Helper, armed officials quickly moved to put that town on lock down. Armed guards went door-to-door throughout the county, seizing firearms as well as members and leaders of the NMU that may have been hiding. During the trials, the NMU's lawyers and representatives would be swarmed and taken out into the desert and beaten as warnings until the ACLU joined the defense. Additionally, some people were combinations of the anti-NMU mob, courtroom guards, and members of the jury. This image, also taken from the 1933 home movie, was filmed in the Price railroad yards. The Utah Oil Refining Company building is visible in the background.

Strife and discord were present in Price very early on. In 1884, brothers Henry George and John Henry Mathis were exploring a series of canyons just north of Price when they stumbled upon the corpse of a man. They loaded the body into their wagon and returned to Price, where Fred E. Grames, the postmaster, wrote a letter asking for help identifying the man who had died by a gunshot wound. The letter was extremely descriptive, right down to the dead man's underwear. The man was identified as "Larson," who was part of a survey party laying out the new town of Price. The canyon was named Deadman's Canyon in his honor and has created local ghostly legends.

On December 7, 1916, tragedy struck when a train collision occurred in the Price railroad yards. A mixed train of freight, coal, and water cars had been fitted with a passenger coach on the end to take passengers from nearby Helper across the county to Sunnyside. The train, known as the *Sunnyside Extra*, had stopped in Price and was performing switching operations when another train that left Helper over an hour later crashed into the back of the passenger car, plowing through the car and coming to a stop in the water cars just ahead.

The engineer of the train that hit the *Sunnyside Extra* reported that the wind had blown the smoke from the engine back into the front of the train, limiting his visibility. Three people were killed, and five were badly injured. The men killed were Tony Verdi and Tony Albo (both Italian immigrants) and William A. Wallace. The engineer of the rear train was held wholly responsible for the crash. With this incident, the *Sunnyside Extra* also earned a position in local supernatural and ghostly legends.

Tony Verdi was an Italian immigrant from Naples who had made a living as a pipe fitter and plumber for the Utah Fuel Company. Verdi was on his way to Sunnyside for business when the crash occurred. Tony left behind his wife, Maria, and nine children, all under the age of 15. This photograph shows Verdi with five of his children.

Tony Verdi's funeral was a grand affair, with a band and a large procession made up of Verdi's fellow Italians. The photograph shows the funeral group as it approaches the hill to the cemetery in Helper. Verdi's home and farm are located just to the left in this photograph.

Another dark episode in Price's history occurred on June 18, 1925. An African American man named Robert Marshall had been sent to the coal mining camps surrounding Price to discuss the formation of labor unions with the National Miners Union (NMU). Marshall was immediately targeted by local and coal mine law enforcement as a black cat communist agitator. On the night of June 15, 1925, Marshall allegedly shot Castle Gate marshal Milton Burns. The three-day manhunt resulted in Marshall being hanged by a lynch mob just east of Price. Eleven men were arrested for the crime, but their cases were dismissed due to lack of evidence, although it is estimated that over 500 people turned out to witness the lynching and postcards of Marshall's body hanging from the tree were sold door-to-door.

Unveiled on March 28, 1910, this was Carbon County Courthouse No. 2. The original courthouse had been much more modest where this one was grand and state of the art. The courthouse was a three-story building crowned with a dome and a cupola. On top of it all was a stunning brass statue of Lady Liberty. A daylong festival on the grounds of the courthouse celebrated its completion. This photograph was taken around 1920.

While the Carbon County Courthouse saw its fair share of exciting legal drama, one of the most highly publicized criminal cases in Utah history took place within its walls. Seventy-four-year-old Hiram BeBee was accused of killing Mt. Pleasant, Utah, marshal Alonzo T. Larsen on October 15, 1945. After BeBee's arrest, rumors started circulating that he was the Sundance Kid. BeBee never claimed that he was the Sundance Kid, but it was repeatedly brought up in his trial in Manti, Utah. BeBee was already targeted for being non-Mormon, and he was never allowed to claim "justifiable self-defense" at his trials.

The trial in Manti was handled so badly that it was deemed a mistrial. The trial was then moved to the courthouse in Price and heard by Judge Fred W. Keller. Keller's rigged court found BeBee guilty of Larsen's killing and sentenced him to death. The sentence was changed to life in prison by the Utah Board of Pardons because of the trial's bias. The trial became a measure for US judicial agencies to determine corrupt trial proceedings. While in prison, Hiram BeBee would often be paraded for the international press like a zoo animal. He died in prison on June 2, 1955, still trying to get a fair trial. This photograph was taken at the Utah State Prison and shows guards removing BeBee's shoes.

While strife was always an issue in Price, there were also good times. At the conclusion of World War II, August 15, 1945, residents of Price flooded the streets for an impromptu victory celebration. World War II had been hard on Price, with hundreds of young men and women leaving to serve their country. Ninety soldiers from Carbon County were killed or are listed as missing. When the victory over Japan was announced, Main Street between Carbon Avenue and 100 East was closed for a huge street party.

At the corner of Main Street and 100 East, Greek residents gathered for some traditional Greek dancing while other members of the community looked on. Local merchants set up radio sets and speakers on the street, and live bands came out to play for the crowd. The war was over, prosperity was once again just around the corner, and Price was celebrating.

The courthouse served the people and corporations of Price until it was torn down in the mid-1950s to make way for a more futuristic, and less attractive looking, courthouse. During the demolition, the brass statue of Lady Liberty was allowed to fall to the ground and break apart on Main Street. The statue was later melted down. People have called it "The Day That Liberty Died in Carbon County." With a bright beam of light illuminating Lady Liberty, this photograph was part of a promotional package for Price. The photograph was taken around 1930.

Six

THE TOWN SHAPED BY EDUCATION

Education was always first and foremost in the minds of the earliest settlers of Price. Although the first school was held in a private home with one very dedicated teacher, it soon became clear that larger, more formal schoolhouses were going to be needed.

Beginning with the Central School in 1901 through the 1950s, Price had numerous elementary schools. Harding School, built in 1925; Notre Dame Catholic School, built in 1927; and Reeves Elementary and Durant Elementary, built in 1954, were used to educate the children of Price.

Once a county high school was established, the student body selected the most unique of all the high school mascots in the nation—the Carbon High School Dinosaurs—and early drawings of Dino have been referred to as a "Darwin's Grab Bag Dino." High school athletics provided a source of pride and joy for the residents, with the football and baseball teams securing Utah state titles several times though out the history of the school. However, it was the band that truly shined. Taking several national titles and working to bring a large, multi-year music festival to Price, the Carbon High School Band was the face of Price's high school.

Not satisfied with ending the education opportunities at high school, Price lobbied to have a college in town, and in 1937, Utah governor Henry H. Blood created Carbon College. Since that time, thousands of students have graduated from the college located in the north end of Price. Throughout the college's name changes, from Carbon College to College of Eastern Utah (CEU) to the present-day Utah State University-Eastern (USU-E), the college in Price has become a world-class facility.

In 1883, the first school was organized and established by Sally Ann Barton Olsen. With the help of her husband, Peter Issac Olsen, Sally became the first teacher in Price a full year before the school district was officially established. The first classes were held at the home of Mathew Simmons. This c. 1884 photograph shows a fairly large school class in Price in front of the LDS Meeting House.

The next school in Price was an adobe brick building later used by the LDS Church for Sunday school. In the summer of 1900, a large brick school was being constructed on a plot of ground northeast of Main Street. Named Central School, classes began in the fall of 1901. An addition was added to the rear portion of the school in 1912. This c. 1908 photograph shows the entire student body, 290 students, at the school.

On the night of January 3, 1915, a fire started in the addition to the Central School. The school was a total loss. Classes were once again returned to the old adobe brick school while a new school building was erected. The new building cost $10,000 to construct and featured large windows, so "harmful light bulbs" would not harm students' eyes. This photograph shows the Central School prior to the fire.

In October 1911, the school district announced that a public high school would be built in Price. The first Carbon County High School was opened in January 1913. The classes at the school focused on career training, with bookkeeping, stenography, and typing classes featured. This photograph shows the school just prior to completion in 1912.

The first dedicated high school in Price was a private school operated by the Methodist Church. Initially held on the top floor of the First National Bank building on the corner of Main Street and 100 West, the church erected a new structure for the school in 1907. The private high school was in operation until 1918, when the church gave the building to the Carbon County High School for use as a dormitory. The dormitory was necessary to house students from the outlying coal camps. The dormitory also housed visiting parents and guest athletic teams. This photograph shows the Methodist school around 1912.

With a large Roman Catholic population in Price, the Very Reverend Monsignor A.F. Giovannoni of the Notre Dame de Lourdes Catholic Church dreamed of having a private, Catholic school for local children. The Notre Dame School opened in 1927. It was not until 1956 that the high school portion of the school was added. This image is a composite photograph showing the Notre Dame School Band as they celebrate their fourth-place win in the school band competition in 1932. High school and elementary school band teacher Edgar Milton "Toot" Williams is pictured on the left, and Monsignor Giovannoni is pictured on the right.

In 1938, Carbon High School was divided into a junior high school serving grades 9 and 10 while the high school students, grades 11 and 12, were combined within the newly opened junior college. The former high school building was made into the junior high school. When the building was occupied by the high school, the school administration placed a cannon in front of it. The cannon pointed directly down Carbon Avenue. School officials always joked that the cannon could be used for defense against Emery County if the need arose. This photograph shows the Carbon High School just after construction was completed around 1913.

The Carbon County High School featured a dedicated industrial arts building. Combined with the commercial students at the high school, the industrial arts students broke away from the commercial guild in 1915 and formed their own group. Classes like this one on woodworking were highly focused on by the school board as well as state educators as they prepared students for real-life careers.

Athletics was always an important part of Carbon County High School. The football teams throughout the history of the high school have won three Utah State Championships, in 1924, 1938, and 1951. This c. 1920 photograph of a pre-game pep rally shows a good play on words with "We Got the Academy's Goat."

A long-standing rivalry between the Carbon County High School and the neighboring Emery County High School is still in place today. Today, when the two teams meet, it is for the right to possess the coal bucket for a year; in the 1920s, it was just for bragging rights. A pre-game pep rally in front of the high school announced "Up With Carbon and Down With Emery," complete with festive Christmas hats.

By the 1930s, Carbon County High School was shortened to Carbon High School, and their school mascot of the Dinosaurs was established. As a point of pride, the students painted a white block letter *C* outlined in blue on the hills behind the high school. The *C* was painted every year by the graduating seniors until the stability of the sandstone on the hill became a concern for school officials. This photograph was taken during a touch-up.

Far and away, the most successful high school organization at Carbon High School was the band. In the 1920s, the Price Chamber of Commerce, along with the Grand Junction, Colorado, Chamber of Commerce, teamed up to promote travel between the two cities. Grand Junction began a band competition, and Price was formally invited to attend. The band traveled to Grand Junction by train and swept the meet, beating 20 other bands to take trophies in every category. Here, the Carbon High School Band poses in front of the Price Carnegie Library with its collection of trophies.

In 1933, the Carbon High School Band performed at the National Band Competition in Evanston, Illinois, after being awarded Utah State Champions in 1932. The band raised money for the excursion, and the Denver & Rio Grande Western Railroad provided three railroad cars for the band members and their parents. The 85-member band wowed the judges and were proclaimed the greatest marching unit ever to enter a national competition. The band brought home first place.

With the success of the band's showing in Grand Junction, Colorado, the Carbon County Chamber of Commerce decided that the competition should be held in Price. The competition was called the Price Intermountain Music Meet, and invitations were sent to bands throughout Utah and western Colorado. The first competition hosted 18 bands with just over 1,000 participants. This c. 1931 photograph shows the Carbon County High School Band.

As the Price Intermountain Music Meet grew, the locals began to call the event "Band Days." By 1937, the Intermountain Band Contest hosted 50 bands and more than 2,500 students over the three-day event. The Denver & Rio Grande Western Railroad offered discounted tickets for the bands traveling to and from Price. Local homes were opened up to house the participants, and businesses put their best faces on. The music competition featured both marching and orchestral competitions as well as solo and ensemble contests. This is the cover of the program from the 1933 competition.

One of the highlights of the competition was the mass band parade. The parade was broken into two parts, with the junior bands leading and the senior bands after them. The bands were judged individually and then collectively as they played a musical selection together. This photograph shows a visiting band preparing to perform on the corner of Main Street and Carbon Avenue.

Author SueAnn Martell's family has a long tradition of band membership in the family; her mother, piccolo player Maurine Greener, poses for a photograph after a Band Days competition in front of the Savoy Hotel on Price's Main Street. Greener was a senior in this photograph taken in 1948. Her older brother Jim had been a trombone player in the 1933 band that won the national competition in Evanston, Illinois. Their sister Virginia had also been a piccolo player with the Carbon High School Band.

One of the reasons that the Carbon High School Band was such a success was that nearly every coal camp school that surrounded Price had its own school bands. These junior bands not only worked hard for their own school, but they were also allowed to participate in the Band Days music competitions in their own divisions. By the time these students entered high school, many of them had been playing in marching bands since fifth grade. This c. 1938 photograph shows a visiting band marching down Carbon Avenue from the high school.

A visiting band passes the Price City Hall and the Carnegie Library during the mass band parade at Band Days. Professional musicians and college music instructors were brought in to judge the competitions. The bands were judged on musical ability, complete instrumentation, and marching techniques.

When the Carbon High School Band swept the music competition in Grand Junction, Colorado, the band from Montrose, Colorado, the reigning competition champions, demanded that the Price band not be allowed back to compete for two years. Carbon High School complied with their request, but to show no ill feelings, the Montrose band and other western Colorado bands were warmly welcomed to Price. The Grand Junction High School Tigers, the Fruita High School Wild Cats, and others all placed well at the Price competition. This photograph shows a visiting band marching past the courthouse.

Another member of the musical Greener family, Darrell Greener played the drums with the Carbon High School Band. While the pinnacle of the band competitions was held in Price during Band Days, the band traveled extensively throughout the state for tournaments as well as to support the athletic teams of Carbon High. This photograph shows Greener preparing to play for an athletic event in northern Utah in 1950. Sadly, Band Days would end a 20-year run a short three years later with the retirement of director Edgar "Toot" Williams.

Although Band Days had come to an end, that was not the end of quality bands to come out of Carbon High School. In 1965, the Carbon High School Band was invited to march in the prestigious Tournament of Roses Parade in Pasadena, California. The band was one of five bands nationwide to participate in the parade. The 104-member band was directed by Glen Fifield and Derral Siggard. This photograph shows the band in action along the parade route on January 1, 1966.

In the mid-1930s, talk began to circulate about creating a junior college in Price. In 1935, the Civic Clubs of Southeastern Utah officially announced its backing of a college to the Utah State Legislature. On February 11, 1937, Carbon College was announced by the legislature and Gov. Henry H. Blood and gratefully accepted by Price mayor J. Bracken Lee. The college opened to classes in October 1938 with 200 students. This c. 1939 photograph shows the main college structure in the foreground, the gymnasium on the left, the industrial arts building behind the main hall, and the track and field behind the buildings.

Prior to the building of Carbon College, a suit was filed in the Utah Supreme Court asking that the State Building Commission "forthwith proceed" with the construction of the college. Opposition to the suit stated that the legislature did not have the authority to spend federal money. Price City officials won the case by stating the delaying tactics by the commission were putting their own federal grant in jeopardy. Construction of the college began in the spring of 1938.

Carbon College was an excellent asset not only to the community of Price, but to the whole of Eastern Utah. Students seeking a higher education now had a choice to stay closer to home. Pictured are, from left to right, Carbon College junior class officers Richard "Dick" Greener (president), Beverly Bithel, John Vatsis, and Donald Dimick in 1942.

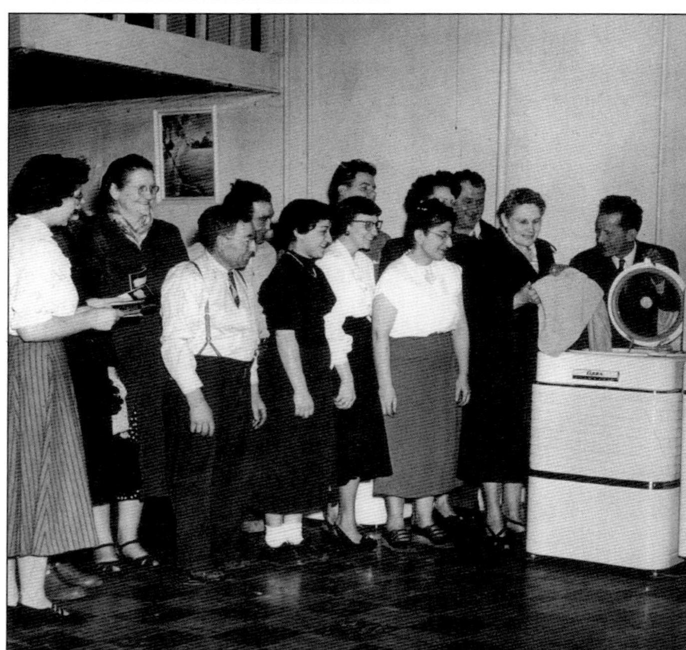

Education in Price came in many different forms. Price businessmen even got into the education game. When Oliveto's Store opened in Price in 1935, representatives of household appliance companies held educational demonstrations for anyone interested in learning the proper way to operate their machines. This class is learning how automatic clothes washers can save time and clean better than other methods.

Seven

The Town Refined by Culture

After a rough-and-tumble start with outlaws and gunfights in the streets and illegal alcohol flowing freely, Price developed quite a large cultural base. Numerous religions reflected the diverse origins of the residents, art and art projects became popular, and, of course, live music and dancing were always available.

There was always something to do in Price, with theaters for both live performances and motion pictures lining each side of Main Street. All of the hit movies of the time were shown here, sometimes on continuous 24-hour screenings. The movie theaters offered patrons confectionaries onsite, where moviegoers could get treats for the show as well as sandwiches, ice cream, and sodas.

Price sought to bring more culture and entertainment by creating its own events. The Robber's Roost Roundup Rodeo and later the Black Diamond Stampede Rodeo drew thousands of people every year. The community festival International Days, started in 1971, continues to draw crowds to experience the culture of the many nationalities that made Price their home.

As a crowning touch, the Carbon College Prehistoric Museum, now the Utah State University Eastern Prehistoric Museum, has welcomed more than one million visitors to Price since its beginnings in 1963. It remains one of the premier museums in Utah and one of the best prehistoric museums in the nation.

For a small, desert settlement with nothing but sagebrush and cactus as far as the eye could see to one of the best culturally diverse cities in eastern Utah, Price has certainly made its mark.

With the first permanent settlers to the Price River Valley being followers of the Church of Jesus Christ of Latter-day Saints, the first community structures also served as Mormon churches and meeting halls. Construction began on the Price tabernacle in 1911, but money was tight, and the building was not actually dedicated until 1924. The tabernacle was in use until the early 1950s, when the building was torn down and the land sold.

Next door to the LDS Tabernacle was the Carbon stake president's office and tithing house. This smaller building was used for the day-to-day operation of the LDS church. It was through this office that funds were raised to go toward the completion of the tabernacle. Church members contributed as much money as they could to the building project, which was estimated to cost just over $50,000. This photograph was taken around 1945.

Completed in August 1916, the Assumption of the Virgin Mary Greek Orthodox Church was dedicated by Rev. Mark Petrakis. The inside of the church is beautifully painted by America's first Greek Orthodox iconographer Theodore Tsavales, uncle to television star Telly Tsavales. Theodore traveled throughout the United States painting most of the Greek churches in America.

The Greek Church in Price was extremely important to the Greek community of Carbon County. While the initial church had been planned for neighboring Helper, where there was a larger population of Greeks, it was decided that the church should be built in Price because of the stronger economic base. The Assumption of the Virgin Mary Greek Orthodox Church has been in use for over 100 years and is the oldest, continuously operated Greek church west of the Mississippi. This c. 1917 photograph shows a group of Greek children attending a service at the church.

When disaster struck within the neighboring coal camps, the ripples were felt throughout the whole of Carbon County. Here, Greek miners who were killed in the March 8, 1924, mine explosion at the nearby Castle Gate coal mine were taken to Price for funeral services in the Greek church. This photograph shows the procession of caskets en route to the Price City Cemetery. The Methodist church is seen in the background.

The first Methodist church in Price was established in 1899. Located on Main Street near Carbon Avenue, the building was a small, white church operated jointly by the Methodists and the Episcopalians. The church began building a new, larger structure in 1923, and it was completed and dedicated in February 1924. This photograph was taken around 1930.

The Catholic church in Price was established by Rev. Alfredo F. Giovannoni, an Italian from Lucca, Italy. After initially leading the church in Helper, Father Giovannoni sought a church in Price. In 1923, the Notre Dame de Lourdes Catholic Church was built in Price. The French name is to honor the French sheepmen in the Price area who contributed so much to the building of the church. The church was also built with the help of volunteer labor. Future Price mayor Rolla E. West built the pulpit by hand. This photograph shows the outside of the church.

Father Giovannoni was reassigned to Salt Lake City in the 1930s. He died on October 5, 1961. The Notre Dame de Lourdes Catholic Church in Price is still in use. Price continues to have a large Catholic population with Italian, Slovenian, French, and Hispanic members. This photograph shows the large rose window in the front of the church.

Live theater and play productions as well as silent movies were a large part of entertainment in early Price. An actor that traveled to Price with his silent film *The Mountain Waif* was Ralph Delmar. Delmar used these hand-signed cards to promote the movie around 1912. Unfortunately, this photograph of Delmar has been repeatedly misidentified as C.L. "Gunplay" Maxwell, a part-time member of the Wild Bunch and bodyguard to attorney Mark P. Braffet. *The Mountain Waif* is now considered to be a lost silent film.

As part of Emmett K. Olsen's push to promote Price, he established a theater on Main Street. Olsen's Eko Theatre initially hosted plays then was remodeled to show silent films. Olsen printed off enlarged photographs of his buildings as well as other scenes throughout Price on large tabloid papers to entice people to move to town and purchase property. This photograph was taken shortly after the Eko opened in 1912.

The perfect example of business diversifying is shown here in this 1915 photograph of the Eko Theatre. Emmett K. Olsen used the upper floor of the theater to open an engineering firm and land office. He also opened the Eko Confectionery on the main floor of the theater. Prior to the Eko Theatre opening, Price had another theater called the Liberty. Olsen is pictured third from the left. This was another one of Olsen's promotional tabloid papers.

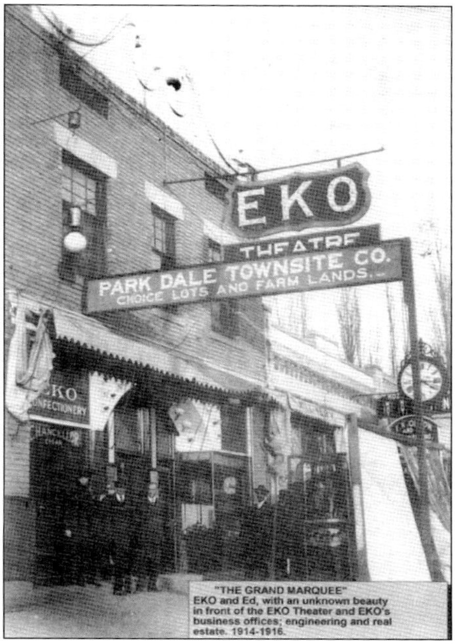

By the early 1930s, the Eko Theatre had changed its name to the Lyric Theater. It was joined in Price by the Bonita, the Star, and, in the late 1930s, the Price Theater. This photograph shows the theater in 1945; it is showing the latest Buster Crabbe film, *Stagecoach Outlaws*. By this time, the theater's name had changed again to the Utah Theater. In 1950, the theater changed its name again to the Crown Theater.

Built in the late 1930s, the Price Theater was located on Main Street one block east of the Eko. The Price Theater was a large building that featured space for businesses on both sides of the theater. This photograph was part of a promotional application applying for housing grants, and it shows the theater in January 1950. The Price Theater is still in operation in its original location. The theater's former owner, Joe Santi, is reported to haunt the theater. Santi mysteriously disappeared after he may have run afoul of the mob.

Theaters were not the only cultural experience one could get in Price. The Silver Moon Dance Hall, shown in this c. 1928 photograph, was located near Price City Park. The Silver Moon was built by John Menotti and provided space for dancing, school proms, special events, and even roller-skating. The building was sold in 1962 to the Kaiser coal mine in nearby Sunnyside, where it was stripped of all of its steel and wiring, which were later repurposed in mining operations.

One of the biggest draws at the Silver Moon Dance Hall was the live orchestras. One of those orchestras was the Night Hawk Orchestra, managed by Leo Leonard. This c. 1924 photograph features, from left to right, Leo Leonard Jr., Calvin A. Jewkes, Clair Leonard, Leo Leonard, Arla Bell Beebe, Lawrence Clayson, George Hawkins, Bob Cormani, Pat Markey, and Emmett Leonard.

In 1939, a new orchestra was organized by a young local drummer named James Dart. Going by the name Jimmy Dart Orchestra, the group began playing in 1940 but disbanded due to World War II. At the conclusion of the war, the band reorganized and played not only in Price, but also throughout Utah and the western United States. This c. 1955 photograph shows a large orchestra. Jimmy Dart is in the second row, third from the right.

Although the orchestra officially called it quits in the 1960s, the members reunited numerous times over the years and even added previous members' children to fill in the empty spots. Dart's wife, Ruth, played the piano in the orchestra, and their children Richard, James Jr., and Diane all played in the orchestra as well. In an interview, Jimmy Dart blamed the popularity of television for the death of big bands. This photograph shows Jimmy behind the drums and Ruth at the piano.

One of the largest events of the summer was the Robber's Roost Roundup Rodeo. The name of the event came from the famous hideout of Butch Cassidy's Wild Bunch. Merchants and residents were asked to dress up in their best Old West attire, and the event was filled with parades, livestock events, and other fun. This c. 1937 photograph shows chuck wagon races at Price City Park.

Organizers of the Robber's Roost Roundup Rodeo initially organized a two-day event, but after the success of the previous two years, the committee added a third day. In 1938, former Wild Bunch member and Carbon County sheriff Matt Warner was grand marshal of the festivities. This photograph was taken in 1939 in front of the new Carbon College as the group prepared for the day's parade.

While the Masonic Lodge had a presence in Price since the early 1900s, the Masons striking three-story temple was not begun until 1923. The cornerstone of the building was laid on December 17, 1923. The building was dedicated and opened on December 11, 1926. The building had both private rooms for Masonic use as well as banquet facilities open to the public. The Price Masonic Temple is still in use today and houses chapters of Free & Accepted Masons (F&AM), Job's Daughters International, and the Eastern Utah Shrine Club.

When the new Price City Hall was completed in 1938, local resident Lynn Fausett was commissioned to paint a mural in the main hallway featuring scenes important to the history of Price. Fausett was born in Price and used historical photographs and personal memories to paint the mural. This photograph shows the "Religion" panel prior to installation in city hall.

Lynn Fausett worked on the mural at the same time as he worked on other projects for the Works Progress Administration (WPA). Fausett designed the tiled arches at the Nebraska State Capitol in Lincoln, Nebraska. Fausett also completed nearly 300 landscape paintings. Due to these other projects, the mural was not completed and installed until November 1941. This panel depicts Chinese immigrants working on the railroad through Price.

Lynn Fausett's health began to decline, and his failing eyesight made artwork difficult. Fausett died on August 17, 1977. This panel depicts Matt Warner enjoying some coffee with the freighters along the Nine Mile Canyon Road. Those using the Nine Mile Route (even the US Calvary out of Fort Duchesne) were known to be escorted by outlaws for protection, thus members of the Wild Bunch in these caravans were not an uncommon sight.

In 1960, a young geologist from Southern California was teaching a night class to several members of the Price community when he said, "You know, you people are crazy! You have the best geology and paleontology in the world right here! You need a museum!" With those words, Donald L. Burge gave birth to one of the world's best paleontological and archaeological museums in the United States. This photograph shows Burge (far right) and founding museum member and local physician Dr. J. Eldon Dorman (second from left). (Courtesy Prehistoric Museum, USU Eastern.)

Dr. J. Eldon Dorman began his career in Utah as a doctor in the coal camps that surrounded Price. As a boy from eastern Colorado, Dorman fell in love with the striking beauty of the desert as well as the outstanding geology and archaeology. Dorman worked with geologists and archaeologists from the University of Utah to get the dream of the museum in motion. An avid amateur archaeologist, Dorman led field trips into the surrounding desert to view rock art. His Jeep safaris were highly anticipated year after year. (Courtesy Prehistoric Museum, USU Eastern.)

In 1961, the museum committee commissioned the Carbon Art League to paint a mural depicting the dinosaur life in eastern Utah during the Jurassic Period. The mural was modeled after *The Age of Reptiles* by Rudolph Zallinger. This photograph shows Don Burge (right) in front of the mural just after the its completion in 1961. (Courtesy Prehistoric Museum, USU Eastern.)

As the centerpiece of the museum, Dr. Dorman and Don Burge wanted a skeleton of an allosaurus excavated from the nearby Cleveland-Lloyd Dinosaur Quarry. The Carbon County Chamber of Commerce spent $2,250 to obtain the skeleton. This photograph shows, from left to right, paleontologist Jim Jensen; Don's wife, Sherril Burge; and Don Burge assembling the allosaurus skeleton at the museum in 1963. (Courtesy Prehistoric Museum, USU Eastern.)

Always active in the field, Don Burge led and participated in numerous dinosaur excavations in the area. He is credited with the discovery of the world-famous Utahraptor with Jim Kirkland, Robert Gaston, and Carl Limone. Burge has a dinosaur named after him, the Gastonia burgei, an armored tank dinosaur from the Cretaceous period. This c. 1965 photograph shows Burge (standing) during an excavation. (Courtesy Prehistoric Museum, USU Eastern.)

Don Burge and Dr. J. Eldon Dorman's dream of a museum came true on June 3, 1961, when a 1,500-square-foot display area opened in a conference room at the Price City Hall. The museum was called the Carbon College Prehistoric Museum. In 1963, when the allosaurus skeleton was completed, it had to be displayed in the hallway because it was so large. This photograph shows Burge and his crew on another dinosaur excavation near Moab, Utah. (Courtesy Prehistoric Museum, USU Eastern.)

Carbon College changed its name and became the independent College of Eastern Utah in 1964. The museum had long outgrown the small conference room, and the Price City Council made the decision to allow the museum to use the city gymnasium as its display space. In 1973, the museum moved into its new space. This photograph shows, from left to right, Dr. J. Eldon Dorman, Prof. Lee Stokes, and Don Burge around 1975. (Courtesy Prehistoric Museum, USU Eastern.)

The museum expanded rapidly through donations and loans made by local citizens. One of the highlights of the exhibits were the numerous dinosaur tracks. Dinosaur tracks are fairly common in the local coal mines, and miners would spend their lunch breaks removing the tracks for the museum display. This c. 1965 photograph shows a woman measuring a large, three-toed dinosaur track on display.

By the late 1980s, the museum was looking to expand again. This time, a new wing was needed. In 1988, construction was started on the addition, west of the existing museum. In 1992, under the direction of Don Burge and the curator of archaeology, Dr. Pam Miller, the College of Eastern Utah Prehistoric Museum received accreditation status from the American Association of Museums. The dream of a small-town tourist attraction had grown into a nationally recognized professional institution. This photograph shows the humble beginnings of the museum in the small conference room at city hall in 1963. (Courtesy Prehistoric Museum, USU Eastern.)

In 1988, one of the most complete Columbian mammoth skeletons was uncovered in nearby Sanpete County. The skeleton was removed to the College of Eastern Utah Prehistoric Museum, where a specialized, climate-controlled room was built to house the specimen. This photograph shows the delivery of a cast of the mammoth skeleton to the area of the college known as the "Bone Lab." The museum is still the jewel in the crown of Price. Now called the Utah State University Eastern Prehistoric Museum, the museum welcomes thousands of visitors annually. (Courtesy Prehistoric Museum, USU Eastern.)

In addition to the Prehistoric Museum, Price also maintains the Bryner Pioneer Museum. Housed inside the home built by settler Albert Bryner in 1892, the Bryner Pioneer Museum not only tells the story of the Bryner family, but also preserves the daily lives of the earliest residents of Price.

Price is in the process of rebuilding itself. There are fewer and fewer coal mines in the surrounding mountains, the railroad does not stop in town anymore, and the city needs to look into other industries to reinvent itself. One way to do that is to look into the past. By preserving Price's wild, unique history and passing this important knowledge on to future generations, tourism and historic preservation are the waves of the future. This photograph shows the authors, SueAnn Martell and Darrin Teply, performing one of their many costumed historical tours, which are officially the longest, continually operating tours of this type in Utah.

The Coal Miner's Memorial, located on the former site of the LDS Tabernacle on Price's Main Street and in front of the Prehistoric Museum, pays tribute to the 1,353 miners killed in coal mines within Carbon County. Dedicated on Labor Day, September 7, 2015, the memorial lists each man killed and the mine they were killed in. The monument was built by donation funds and volunteers who dedicated their time to research the data.